Praise for John Elder Robison's
Look Me in the Eye

"There's an endearing quality to Robison and his story. . . . *Look Me in the Eye* is often drolly funny and seldom angry or self-pitying. Even when describing his fear that he'd grow up to be a sociopathic killer, Robison **brings a light touch to what could be construed as dark subject matter**. . . . Robison is also **a natural storyteller and engaging conversationalist**."
> —*Boston Globe*

"Of course this book is brilliant; my big brother wrote it. But even if it hadn't been created by my big, lumbering, swearing, unshaven 'early man' sibling, this is as sweet and funny and sad and true and heartfelt a memoir as one could find, utterly unspoiled, uninfluenced, and original."
> —AUGUSTEN BURROUGHS

"Deeply felt and often darkly funny, *Look Me in the Eye* is a delight."
> —*People* (Critic's Choice)

"A fantastic life story told with grace, humor, and a bracing lack of sentimentality."
> —*Entertainment Weekly*

"Not only does Robison share with his famous brother, Augusten Burroughs (*Running with Scissors*),

a talent for writing; he also has that same deadpan, biting humor that's so irresistible."

—*ELLE*

"Robison seems likable, honest, and completely free of guile, qualities well served by writing that is lean, powerful in its descriptive accuracy and engaging in its understated humor. . . . **Emotionally gripping.**"

—*Chicago Tribune*

"John Robison's book is **an immensely affecting account of a life lived according to his gifts rather than his limitations.** His story provides ample evidence for my belief that individuals on the autistic spectrum are just as capable of rich and productive lives as anyone else."

—DANIEL TAMMET, author of *Born on a Blue Day: Inside the Extraordinary Mind of an Autistic Savant*

"This is no misery memoir. . . . **[Robison] is a gifted storyteller with a deadpan sense of humor and the book is a rollicking read.**"

—*Times* (London)

"Robison's lack of finesse with language is not only forgivable, but **an asset to his story.** . . . His rigid sentences are arguably more telling of his condition than if he had created the most graceful prose this side of Proust."

—*Chicago Sun-Times*

"I hugely enjoyed reading *Look Me in the Eye*. This book is **a wild roller-coaster ride.**"

—TEMPLE GRANDIN, author of *Thinking in Pictures*

"***Look Me in the Eye* is a fantastic read** that takes readers into the mind of an Aspergian both through its plot and through the calm, logical style in which Robison writes. **Parents of children with Asperger's or other forms of autism may find it inspiring that a fellow Aspergian overcame a difficult childhood to lead an exciting, fulfilling life like Robison's.** But even if you have no personal connections with Asperger's, **you'll find that Robison—like his brother, Burroughs—has a life worth reading about.**"

—*Daily Camera* (Boulder)

"An **entertaining, provocative, and highly readable story** by a great storyteller who happens to have Asperger's . . . By the time Mr. Robison's story is finished, **you will rethink your own definition of normal,** and it may spark a new appreciation of the untapped potential behind every quirky, awkward person who doesn't quite fit in."

—TARA PARKER-POPE, "Well," NYTimes.com

"*Look Me in the Eye* is **a wonderful surprise on so many levels: it is compassionate, funny, and deeply insightful.** By the end, I realized my vision of the world had undergone a slight but permanent alteration; I had taken for granted that our behavioral conventions were meaningful, when in fact they are arbitrary. That he is able to illuminate something so simple (but hidden, and unalterable) proves that John Elder **Robison is at least as good a writer as he is an engineer, if not better.**"

—HAVEN KIMMEL, author of *A Girl Named Zippy*

Be Different

Also by John Elder Robison

Look Me in the Eye

Be Different

My Adventures with Asperger's
and My Advice for Fellow Aspergians, Misfits,
Families, and Teachers

John Elder Robison

BROADWAY PAPERBACKS

NEW YORK

BROADWAY

Broadway Paperbacks and its logo, a letter B bisected on the diagonal,
are trademarks of Random House, Inc.

Originally published in hardcover in the United States by
Crown Archetype, an imprint of the Crown Publishing Group,
a division of Random House, Inc., New York, in 2011.

Library of Congress Cataloging-in-Publication Data

Robison, John Elder.
  Be different : my adventures with Asperger's and
my advice for fellow Aspergians, misfits, families,
and teachers / John Elder Robison. — 1st ed.
  1. Asperger's syndrome.   2. Difference (Psychology)
3. Marginality, Social.   4. Individual differences.
5. Robison, John Elder.   I. Title.

  RC553.A88R63 2011
  616.85'8832—dc22

                                       2010053205

ISBN 978-0-307-88482-4
eISBN 978-0-307-88483-1

Printed in the United States of America

Book design by Lauren Dong
Cover photography © PM Images/Getty Images

10 9 8 7 6 5 4 3 2

First Paperback Edition

For my son, Cubby,
the very embodiment of being different

Contents

Contents

Be Different

Introduction

MADISON SQUARE GARDEN, 1979. *The New York concert was the high point of KISS's Dynasty tour, and we kicked it off with a bang and a flash. The band played loud enough to make your ears bleed, and our pyrotechnics would burn your eyebrows off if you got too close. We were five songs into the set. "Firehouse" had just ended. We killed the spotlights and got to work. Buzzes and clicks from the sound system suggested activity up on the blackened stage. The applause was over, and low ripples of noise washed through the audience as they waited for the next song.*

We had less than two minutes to make the change, and I'd prepared all day so I'd be ready to go when the lights went down. The crowd was calm; no one had started chanting. Yet. I had no intention of letting that mob of twenty thousand fans get restless, so I moved as quickly as I could. It was only a short jump for them to move from lighting matches and chanting to lighting the place on fire, so I finished up fast, before anything else could happen. I scampered off the edge of the stage as the musicians took their places in the dark.

I turned around just in time to hear a pop followed by a flash of hard white light from stage left. The opening chords of "New York Groove" barked out as Ace Frehley turned to face the crowd. The main stage was still dark; a single spotlight illuminated KISS's lead guitarist as he stood alone to play the opening riff. He'd been using an ordinary black Les Paul guitar for the past few songs. Now he held something different—something alive. The face of his instrument had transformed into a mirror glittering with a thousand lights. They moved and rippled in concert with the notes he played, a pattern of light that reached all the way to the back of the Garden.

It was a guitar unlike any other. Even the sound was different. It had a hard metallic bite; and the sound of the strings was punctuated by ticks as the lights flashed beneath them. No one had seen anything remotely like that before.

The crowd went wild as Ace's light swept over them in time to the music. The traditional order was suddenly turned upside down. At every concert before, spotlights had illuminated the stage. Tonight, a musician made his own light, and threw it out over the audience. For that brief moment, in the face of all of KISS's rock-and-roll thunder, simple radiance had stolen the show.

It was my light shining from that stage. I had created that guitar, and many others, while working with rock-and-roll bands. I was twenty-two years old.

That is a memory I cherish; one I know was made possible by Asperger's syndrome, a difference inside my brain. I developed the skills to create that guitar only because of those differences.

I love to think back on my time touring with KISS, but I have many other, more painful, memories that I've pushed to the back of my mind. I've moved on from my anxiety-ridden childhood, a time when I wasn't sure if I'd ever "make it." In the years since, I've proven to myself and to the world that through hard work, patience, diligence, and good fortune I could overcome the obstacles life, and my Aspergian brain, put in my path. I grew up to be a master musical technician, a business owner, an author, a father, and, most important, a functioning adult who is valued by his family, his friends, and society.

Repressed memories of tougher times and the emotions associated with them may still come flooding back unexpectedly, spurred by an episode or event. That's exactly what happened a few years ago as I watched *Billy the Kid,* a documentary about an undiagnosed Aspergian sixteen-year-old in a small-town Maine high school.

In one scene, Billy moves warily among his classmates. As he walks the halls, you see his eyes dart from side to side. Constantly. Looking for threats. Like a lone deer in a forest filled with wolves. With a pang, I recognized his look the moment I saw it. That was me, in tenth grade, at Amherst High. Seeing his face, I experienced all the worry and anxiety of that time in my life in an instant. I knew exactly how he felt. Alone, scared. Sure no one around him understood him; not even sure if he understood himself.

A few weeks later, I showed the film to a therapist friend, who dismissed Billy's look with a pat explanation. "I've seen that before," he said. "They call it furtive eye movements. It's common in people on the autism spectrum. It doesn't mean anything."

It doesn't mean anything. I felt like I'd been punched in the gut. When it comes to human interactions, I can't think of a single instance where that is true. Every expression and gesture means something. It's sometimes hard to figure out what the meaning is, but it always exists.

> It doesn't mean anything. *I felt like I'd been punched in the gut.*

I didn't need any help figuring out what Billy was feeling. I have felt the same thing myself, too many times. He was wary, scanning the cafeteria continuously, watching for threats, just as I had done in high school. With a sense of certainty that's rare in the world of psychology, I knew the therapist was wrong.

Realizing that I had insight into what Billy was feeling, insight that a professional therapist, whom I trusted, didn't have, confirmed that I had to share my journey with others. Individuals are labeled "different," "geeky," "abnormal," or even "Aspergian" or "autistic" at a young age. Among other things, these labels suggest that the people around them—their family, friends, teachers, and counselors—can't relate to their actions and expressions.

That's understandable, but it doesn't mean that those actions aren't motivated by legitimate feelings and desires, or that those of us who are different aren't capable of achieving amazing things in our lifetime. There's so much talk about the disability of Asperger's, so much focus on what kids who are different can't do, that I thought it was time for a book about what they CAN do.

Thanks to my Asperger's, I didn't have much luck making friends as a kid. I always said or did the wrong thing. Grown-ups, especially teachers, didn't know what to make of me. They knew I was smart, so they didn't understand why I misbehaved and never fit in. I couldn't do anything the way people told me to, which caused a ton of conflict. I had to find my own way.

If my teachers wouldn't, or couldn't, teach me, I figured, I'd have to teach myself. And that's exactly what I did. I learned from watching people, from reading a lot, and from experimentation. I developed tricks to overcome my weaknesses and exploit my strengths. The skills I've learned along the way, and my techniques for acquiring them in the first place, became the basis of this book.

Despite a difficult childhood, I've achieved quite a few of the things regular people aspire to do, accomplishments that make me sound pretty normal. The thing is, because of my Asperger's, my path to accomplishing those things ended up being a little different from the normal route; actually, it ended up a LOT different. But I still reached goals anyone, different or not, would be proud to achieve.

If you were recently diagnosed with Asperger's, or you have a child with Asperger's, or you work with Asperger children or just plain geeky kids in schools or elsewhere, this is the book for you. I wrote *Be Different* because the existing prescriptive works on Asperger's were—to be frank—mostly clinical and/or depressing. Not this one. I believe those of us with Asperger's are here for a reason, and we have much to offer. This book will help you bring out those gifts.

My stories will focus on me, a guy with Asperger's, but even if you don't share my diagnosis, you may still relate to these tales. Millions of people with ADHD, ADD, or any form of autism, and even common geeks, share many of my traits. After all, everyone feels like an outsider some of the time.

I certainly hope reading my stories and learning about the ways I coped with problems and found my path entertain you while also giving some useful insights into dealing with your own quirks, or those of someone you care about.

Asperger's and Me

Asperger's came into my life when I was forty years old. I'm a pretty levelheaded guy, but I was totally shocked by the diagnosis. "Yep," the doctors said, "you were born this way." I could not believe I had reached middle age without knowing such a hugely important thing about myself. I was amazed to learn that Asperger's is a kind of autism, because I thought everyone with autism was disabled. I'd always envisioned myself as a loner, a geek, and a misfit, but I would never have described myself as disabled. To me, being disabled meant having no legs or being unable to talk. Yet

Asperger's was a disability—that's what the books said. I'm still not sure I believe that.

autism, and so Asperger's, was a disability—that's what the books said. I'm still not sure I believe that.

The one shred of reassurance I got that first day was the knowledge that Asperger's isn't a terminal illness. "You're not getting sicker," they told me, "and it won't kill you. You're actually not sick at all; you're just different." *Great*, I thought. *Very comforting.*

All of a sudden, the concept of "people like me" took on a whole new meaning. Moments before, I'd have described myself as a middle-aged white male. I was a successful business owner, a husband, and a father. Now I was a guy with Asperger's. I was autistic. Everything else seemed secondary to that new facet of me. *This must be how it feels when you find you have cancer,* I thought. I was still the same guy I had been the day before. I didn't feel sick. Yet somehow, in a matter of seconds, my diagnosis had come to dominate my self-image.

In the weeks that followed, I read everything I could about the diagnosis, and I began to relax. When I thought back on my life, Asperger's explained so many things. School had been hard for me, and I'd done some pretty unusual stuff after dropping out. My new knowledge of Asperger's brought those memories into focus, and I saw how the differences in my brain had shaped the course of my life in countless subtle ways. Yet I also realized that the success I enjoyed as an adult was real, and it wasn't going away. In fact, as I moved forward with new knowledge and confidence, I started to see my life get better every day.

Later, with the benefit of this new knowledge, I studied my Aspergian son, now twenty-one years old, and thought about how he too used to struggle in school and in social settings. He was diagnosed when he was sixteen, twenty-four years earlier than me. I look at him today, and I see how much he's benefited from understanding how and why his brain is different from other folks'. In many ways, he's the young man I could have been if only I had known what I had. I made it through life the hard way; he has the benefit of knowledge to rely on. That will make his path easier, and it can make yours easier, too.

Observed from the outside, Asperger's is a series of quirks and behavioral aberrations. Aspergians are not physically disabled, though an observant person might pick us out of a crowd by our unusual gait or even by our expressions. Most Aspergians possess all the body parts and basic abilities for the full range of human functions. We're also complete on the inside. When today's brain scientists talk Asperger's, there's no mention of damage— just difference. Neurologists have not identified anything that's missing or ruined in the Asperger brain. That's a very important fact. We are not like the unfortunate people who've lost millions of neurons through strokes, drinking, lead poisoning, or accidental injury. Our brains are complete; it's just the interconnections that are different.

All people with autism have some kind of communication impairment. "Traditional" autistic people have trouble understanding or speaking language. If you can't talk, or understand others, you are indeed going to be disabled in our society. The degree of impairment can vary greatly, with some autistic people totally devoid of speech and others affected in less substantial ways.

Autistic people can also have impairment in the ability to read nonverbal signals from others. That's the kind of autism I have; it's what most people with Asperger's are touched with. The stories in this book describe the ways in which I minimized the harm my communication impairment caused me, while finding the gifts it conferred.

Autism in its many forms is not a disease. It's a way of being that comes from this nonstandard wiring in the brain. The latest science suggests we're most likely born different, or else we become autistic early in infancy. We don't develop Asperger's as teenagers; life on the autism spectrum is the only life we've ever known. We will always be perplexed when we gaze at people who aren't on the spectrum, and they will always struggle to understand our unconventional way of thinking.

Subtle brain differences often cause people like me to respond differently—strangely even—to common life situations. Most of us have a hard time with social situations; some of us feel downright crippled. We get frustrated because we're so good at some things, while being completely inept at others. There's just no balance. It's a very difficult way to live, because our strengths seem to contrast so sharply with our weaknesses. "You read so well, and you're so smart! I can't believe you can't do what I told you. You must be faking!" I heard that a lot as a kid.

Some people with autism are noticeably disabled. A person who can't talk, for example, cries out for compassion. Those of us with Asperger's are tougher to pick out.

The hardest thing about having Asperger's is that we don't look any different from anyone else on the outside. So why would anyone suspect that we are different on the inside? When I was a kid, no one had any knowledge of how my brain was wired, including me. Consequently, society wrote me off as defective along with millions of other "different" and "difficult" children. My strange behavior was described as "bad" instead of being seen for what it was—the innocent result of neurological difference.

Today most kids are diagnosed earlier than I was, but still, for many of us, knowledge of Asperger's starts with some kind of failure. Most kids get diagnosed with Asperger's after failing at some aspect of school, and their behavior has brought them to the attention of the little men in suits who give tests.

I may not have been tested in school, but the differences in me were still obvious. I could not make friends, I acted strange, and I flunked all my courses. Back then, people said I was just a bad kid, but today we see problems like mine as evidence of disability, and, as a society, we supply help, not punishment. At least, that's how it's supposed to work.

Today, many geeks, scientists, and other creative geniuses are said to have Asperger's. But to some of us, the phrase "have Asperger's" is misleading because it makes Asperger's sound like a disease or an injury. You say, "I have a cold" or "I've got a broken leg." Saying you "have" something implies that it's temporary and undesirable.

Asperger's isn't like that. You've been Aspergian as long as you can remember, and you'll be that way all your life. It's a way of being, not a disease.

That's why I say, "I am a person with Asperger's."

Many of us shorten this by saying we're Aspergians, or Aspies. I think that's more appropriate than saying, "We have Asperger's." There's no right or wrong—you can say whatever you want, or say nothing at all. Whatever you choose, you're in good company. Bill Gates is said to be Aspergian. Musician Glenn Gould is said to have been Aspergian, along with scientist Albert Einstein, actor Dan Aykroyd, writer Isaac Asimov, and movie director Alfred Hitchcock. As adults, none of those people would be described as disabled, but they were certainly eccentric and different.

If everyone with Asperger's achieved a high level of success, no one would call it a disability. Unfortunately, those people are the exceptions, not the rule. Most Aspergians struggle with school, relationships, and jobs because their social skills are poor and they can't seem to fit in. It's all too easy to end up alone, alienated, and unemployed. That's what life

My differences turned out also to include gifts that set me apart.

was like for me before I learned how to work with my differences, overcome them, and sometimes exploit them. As I have gotten older, I have come to appreciate how my differences have turned out also to include gifts that have set me apart. One of my main goals in life today is to help young people avoid some of the traps I fell into. We should all be given a chance to succeed.

There's a lot more to this story than simple disability.

The Three Categories: Aspergian, Proto-Aspergian, and Nypical

Sometimes people say, "I see myself in your stories, but I don't have an Asperger diagnosis. Why is that?" Well, I have my theories. . . .

As we now know, Asperger's is part of a broad spectrum of human behavior, with extremely disabled autistic people at one end and the teeming mass of undiagnosed humanity at the other. All of us fall somewhere on this imaginary behavioral continuum. In fact, it seems to me that there are really only three kinds of people in the world, each grouped on a different arc of the spectrum.

> *All of us fall somewhere on this imaginary behavioral continuum.*

First are those of us with an autism or Asperger diagnosis. At a little over one percent of the population, we are the smallest group, but we are special and attract notice far beyond what our numbers would suggest. We're the ones who are officially "on the autism spectrum," and there is tremendous variation among us. Some of us can't function without assistance, while others are incredibly gifted. Taken together, we may not seem like we have a single thing in common, but we do—we share subtle structural differences in our brains that make us autistic.

I call the next group proto-Aspergians. These are people with plenty of Asperger quirks but not too many disabilities. They're different and eccentric, but most of them blend into society a bit more smoothly than we full-blooded Aspergians do. There are quite a few proto-Aspergians out there—perhaps as much as five percent of the population. Lots of engineers, scientists, geeks, and common nerds are in this category—that is, unless they qualify for the Diagnosis to put them in the first group. Many are blessed with above-average intelligence, and most are pretty functional. Some people say the proto-Aspergians are the ones who were born with all the benefits of Asperger's without any of the bad stuff. Perhaps that's true.

Proto-Aspergians are also called geeks or nerds. Every school has a bunch—the people with lots of Asperger-like traits but not so many as to be labeled. Some proto-Aspergians have alternate diagnoses, like ADHD. Others are just eccentric. They populate the Math Club, the computer room, the Science Fiction Society, and other such places. As grown-ups, they can be found in technology companies, universities, online gaming groups, and even car-repair shops like mine. They are everywhere. Who knows—you may be one of them. I didn't learn about

Asperger's until I was forty years old, but I knew about geeks right from the beginning. Geeks have always been around.

The third group contains everyone else. But what should we call them? If people with Asperger's are called Aspergians or Aspies, it makes sense that we would need a special name for people who don't have Asperger's and aren't proto-Aspergian. "People who don't have Asperger's" sounds pretty clumsy when you say it too often. "Everyone else" is too vague. You might think the correct word would be "normal," but we've all heard the psychologist's pronouncement "There is no such thing as normal."

Professionals have coined the word "neurotypical" to describe any human who does not have some form of autism. "Neurotypical" has been in use for a number of years, but I've never liked it. Try it yourself. Say it in front of a mirror and watch your mouth. It's like you're chewing something just to spit the syllables out. It's so clinical—you can almost smell the doctor's office when you say it.

"Neurotypical" is the kind of word you hear in science fiction movies, when they select the specimens for dissection. I wanted a friendlier word, something that didn't remind me of tongue depressors and needles. I wanted a word I wouldn't stumble over if I said it late at night. So I made my own contraction, "nypical."

That's right. Nypical. Pronounced NIP-ick-al. Now you say it.

The word rhymes with "typical." In fact, you could use the words together. As in, "You're a typical nypical!"

So welcome to nypicality, in all of its wondrous variation. And if you are a nypical . . . get used to it. Now you too have a label to live with.

And it's not all bad. As a nypical, you are part of the majority. And what a majority it is! When we have a majority in political elections, the winner's share of the vote is fifty-five percent. When the share reaches seventy-five percent, it's called a landslide. The share of nypicality is more than ninety-four percent. What more could you ask for?

Everyone fits into one of three groups. Which one is right for you?

If you can't be a proud Aspergian, it's the next best thing to be . . . a nypical.

And there you have it. The three kinds of humanity: people on the spectrum, proto-Aspergians, and the nypical masses. Everyone fits into one of those three groups. Which one is right for you?

Finding Your Path to "Fitting In"

Those of us with Asperger's will always have different brains, but I firmly believe that different does not have to mean disabled. Many Aspergians—me included—were somewhat disabled as children, but with a strategy, hard work, determination, and the acquisition of hard-won wisdom, we overcame our disabilities to emerge as successful and capable adults. My own life story illustrates that clearly.

When I was young, I could not make friends. I couldn't play in groups. At school, I didn't do assignments the way I was told, and I ended up flunking out. I became a juvenile delinquent. Those are all signs of failure. That's what psychologists look for when deciding if you have a disability. If you're eccentric or even weird, but you're not failing at work or in your personal life, you are not disabled. You're just different. It's only when you fail at some key thing—as I did—that you become "officially" disabled. In my case, the disability was a result of my Asperger's. My different brain just would not permit me to conform to the mold my teachers and other kids wanted to stuff me into.

In many ways, my Asperger's set me up for failure in my early years. Luckily, the state of failure wasn't permanent. I wanted to fit in and succeed, and I worked hard to learn to get along. I taught myself the basics of reading other people. I learned how to divine what people expected of me, and I learned how to deliver on that while still staying true to my own beliefs.

My strategy worked. Today, I'm quite successful, and the same Asperger traits that made me a failure as a kid have played a large part in facilitating my success as an adult. The brain differences that made it difficult for me to interact with people actually helped me to concentrate on other things, like machines.

Failure doesn't have to be permanent.

That concentration led me to develop abilities with machines that others don't have, and I've been very successful in using those skills to advance my career. That's really a good example of how something that seems like a pure disability can actually have components of a gift, too. That was true for me, and it can be true for you, too.

I sure wish someone could have told me that when I was in fourth grade. Back then, schools didn't even know what Asperger's was, let alone what to do for a kid who had it. The whole concept of special education and accommodations was just emerging. Even today, few people can chart a path from failure to success for an Aspergian child. That's why I wrote this book—to show the steps that took me from being a floundering ten-year-old to a successful adult.

The brain differences that make us Aspergian never go away, but we can learn two important things: how to play to our strengths and what to do to fit in with society. Both those skills will lead to a vastly improved quality of life. Actually, you could say every human has to learn those same things, but it's more critical for those of us who are what you might call "nonstandard." For us, learning is not as instinctive and easy as we might wish.

Learning how to fit in does not change any of the Aspergian qualities of our brains. If at age ten you have the unique ability to tell someone what day of the week he was born on, you'll probably still have that ability at age thirty. The difference is, if you learned to fit in, you'll probably have a lot more friends when you're older, and the world will see you in a different light because you relate to others better. That, at least, is the goal.

Psychologists lump all that practice and knowledge under the heading "social skills." Whatever you call it, learning how to get along with other people is vital for our own success and happiness. There's even a fancy psychological theory for that. It's called the "competence-deviance hypothesis." Here's what it says:

When you are young, you have not yet made a reputation in your community. You're an unknown quantity. If you act strange, people will be very wary because they don't know what to make of you. They'll be quick to assume you belong in a cage, under restraint. Later in life, once you build a reputation for competence, the same strange behavior will be dismissed as harmless eccentricity. So the stuff that gets you chased out of town at sixteen gets laughed off at forty-six. In adulthood, the focus shifts from superficial attributes to your actual accomplishments. That's a much better place for an Aspergian, because our sharply focused intelligence often gives us special abilities.

I have certainly seen that in my own life. People today ask me questions about a wide range of topics, and they take my answers quite seriously. Twenty years ago, most people would not consider my opinion at all, and if I voiced one anyway, they'd say, "You're nuts!" The difference between then and now—as best I can tell—is that I have established a name for myself; I have demonstrated my competence to the world, and I am therefore credible. There's another important difference: I learned to get along with other people. The quality of my thought at age thirty or even at age fifteen was not one bit lower, but no one knew who I was. I didn't get any smarter, but I grew and changed in other ways, and that's what made the difference.

Distilled down to one sentence, you can say: Competence excuses strange behavior. That's a very important point for those of us on the spectrum, because our special interests can make us extremely competent in whatever we find fascinating. At the same time, our Asperger's often makes us look pretty strange to outsiders.

Some of the changes that help us fit in better occur naturally as we get older. That's the nature of Asperger's—it produces what psychologists call "developmental delays." We're slow to pick up some social skills, and we'll never be perfect at using them, but most of us can learn enough to get by. While all of us grow and develop our entire lives, the pace of development slows down for most people in the late teen

> *Competence excuses strange behavior.*

years. That's when those of us with Asperger's get our chance to catch up. Catching up may be a lot of work, but with sufficient focus and resolve, it can be done. So a kid whose social skills were way behind his peers in seventh grade may end up being just a little eccentric in college, and downright popular in middle age.

Always keep this point in mind: the word "delay" means what it says: late. Delayed isn't never, no matter how much it may feel like that at age fifteen or even twenty-five.

When we do finally start catching up it makes us feel good. We feel successful. At the same time, we may be at an age when we are beginning to discover some of our Aspergian gifts. And let's be clear about something—we all have these gifts. I don't mean we're all geniuses; I simply mean that each of us has something he or she is particularly good at. Depression and attitude can rob us of the ability to see our gifts, but they absolutely reside in all of us. Since we Aspergians think differently, we're likely to have special or unusual skills, and it's important to find them.

When we discover and build upon our gifts it spurs positive feelings in us and those around us, and those feelings go a long way toward dissipating the burden of failure that many young Aspergians carry as kids. That alone will make us more successful, because positive attitudes translate to positive results. Success breeds success, just as failure breeds failure. When we feel successful we're less likely to melt down or lash out at other people, and we get along better socially. As we make friends we become happier, and it starts a cycle of positive reinforcement. I think that's a key factor to help us avoid slipping into depression.

Find life and work settings that minimize your weaknesses, and you discover your strengths and play to them.

When we get older, we acquire more knowledge and our ability to understand abstract concepts improves. Few six-year-olds understand the concept of a neurological difference, but at sixteen, most can get it. If my own life is any guide, understanding how and why we are different is essential to knowing how we need to change for a better life. That understanding comes with increased maturity.

In my experience, that is the path from disabled to gifted. You learn social skills. You find life and work settings that minimize your weaknesses, and you discover your strengths and play to them. It sounds easy, set out like that, but it entails a huge amount of work. It's been a lifetime job for me, but the results are worth it all.

I hope my stories will give you some ideas.

Part 1

Rituals, Manners, and Quirks

One of the things you hear about often, when you learn about Asperger's and autism, is that we have "restricted and repetitive patterns of behavior and interests." If you're new to this world, you probably wonder what that phrase means.

For some of us, that may mean sitting at a table, stacking and unstacking the same four pencils for hours on end. It may mean repeating a phrase or passage from a song endlessly, until everyone in earshot is ready to explode. And the interests . . . they can run the gamut from knowing the name of every saxophone player in the world of jazz to calculating all the prime numbers with fewer than five digits, to total mastery of Warcraft or another online world. Like everything in the world of autism, these rituals and routines come in all shades and degrees. Some rituals hold you back; others are merely annoying. Routines and fixations that are annoying in children can turn into gifts, if you can find employment that uses the particular need for routine.

In these next stories, I've tried to bring that dry diagnostic passage to life with some examples from my own youth.

For the Love of Routine

I sure love routine and ritual. It's the way of my world. Everything has to be just so. As a toddler, I lined up my blocks a certain way, and, in my mind, that was the only possible way those blocks could be laid out. Any other arrangement of blocks was simply wrong and had to be corrected. It never occurred to me that other kids could have their own ideas about block arranging. Maybe that's one reason I didn't have too many friends back then.

> *I learned to accept the way other people do things even when I'm sure that they are wrong.*

Even today, when I can intellectually grasp the idea that blocks can be stacked and lined up in many different ways, and even heaped or piled, there is still just one way for me. I know other people have their own ideas, but that doesn't make them right. At least, not to me.

But I learned a secret along the way. I learned to accept

the way other people do things even when I'm sure that they are wrong. By learning to let other people make their own choices, and their own mistakes, I avoided antagonizing them and I stopped making enemies for no good reason. It took a while, but I finally came to see that block piling was not something worth fighting over. Most of the time.

There are equivalents to that in adult life, too, and I've learned to treat them the same. I know you should never unplug your computer by yanking the cord, but I've learned to keep quiet when my friend George does it. For that reason, and a few others, he has remained my friend through many years and countless power cords. All that time, he has remained blissfully ignorant, and indeed he's come to accept that six months is a long life for an electrical cord. For him.

Growing up, I always assumed that other kids were like me, that they saw the wisdom in my rituals as much as I did. There was big trouble if anyone tried to change my routines. I'd holler and yell and cry. Now I know better—each person wants to make his or her own decisions about how to act. Some people have rituals like I do, and others don't. I still get uncomfortable if someone questions or disturbs my habits, but I'm able to avoid a meltdown.

I continue to have little rituals today. Some of them make sense to other people, while others seem nutty. But now that I've gotten older and have made a place for myself in the community, people don't usually criticize me for them. For example, I'll go to the same restaurant, sit in the same seat, and order the same food every day. To me, that's perfectly normal and comforting. No one at the restaurant ever complains. In fact, they think it's great. They even have a term for people like me—"regular customers." If I had done that when I was a kid, though, people would have called it weird. So which is it, weird or regular?

One thing I have noticed about restaurants is that the staff never criticizes your rituals, even if they are rude. You can eat with your fingers or even pick your nose, and no one will say anything. If you're a kid who has lived with a lot of criticism, that can be very liberating. However, it can also leave you with a false sense of security, because you get comfortable with some behavior and it comes back to kick you in the teeth in a different setting. That happened to me when I dined with my friend Amy when I was eighteen and new to living on my own.

I met Amy Margulies just after I'd moved in with the guys from Fat, the rock-and-roll band I joined when I left home in the mid-1970s. The musicians in the band and I occupied a big communal house in rural Ashfield, Massachusetts. Amy was a college student who rented a room in a house up the street. I can't imagine what she saw in me, but there must have been something there, because she invited me out to dinner. It's possible she believed that my life with a bunch of traveling musicians was exciting. I was sure the reality would disappoint her, but it was still a date with a real live girl, so I seized the moment. We headed to the Whale Inn, a grand but run-down old place about five miles from where we lived.

By that time, I had been eating out for years. It had started in high school, when I went to the Hungry U or Pizza Rama for lunch every day. As my family situation got worse and my income grew, I began eating dinners out, too, mostly pepper-and-onion pizzas with cherry cola. I didn't have much experience with fancy places like the Whale Inn, but I wanted to impress Amy, so off we went.

Amy's father worked for the government and she had traveled all over the world. She was from a respectable family where—according to her—everyone was polite and well-mannered.

We ordered dinner, which included vegetables served "family-style." Family-style is a way of piling all the stuff on a single plate to save the cooks the effort of sorting and arranging individual portions. On this fateful night, the pile included asparagus, potatoes, and some silver-dollar-sized slices of whitish plant matter with a waxy-looking yellow outer covering.

Perhaps my quizzical look was obvious, because Amy said, "Those are squash. They're good!" I did not say anything, but I watched closely to see if she ate any of the so-called squash, and if so, how. Some foods with outer coverings, like sausages, hot dogs, and chocolate-covered raisins, are eaten whole. But then there are other foods like fancy cheese where the covering has to be removed.

Looking at the strange white disks on the plate, it was hard to tell if the yellow covering was natural or ornamental plastic. And even if it was natural, it still might not be edible. I had previously made that mistake with the covering on shrimp. The outer shell of a shrimp is nasty—nothing like the chocolate covering on a raisin.

I knew this was a potential trap, one where I might either eat something totally repulsive or do something completely ridiculous. So I did nothing but watch. She didn't eat any squash, which led me to question whether the whole thing was a joke. Chinese restaurants do stuff like that. They put brightly colored plant garnishes on top of your Oriental Delight, but if you eat the colored stuff it's like you just ingested cherry-and-spearmint wood chips.

Suspecting a trick, I decided to take the safe way out and eat the asparagus. I'd eaten asparagus for as long as I could remember, and I liked it, especially when it was fresh. I had a system for consuming the stuff: I'd pick up a piece with my thumb and forefinger, holding it about two inches from the base. If it stayed rigid, it was okay to eat. If it flopped over, it was rotten or overcooked. Pieces that failed the test were discarded.

This asparagus stayed firm, so I moved it toward my mouth. With a quick snap I bit off the tip, which is the best part. Asparagus is best when it's minced, so I worked my teeth like a gasoline-powered hedge clipper as I continued to slide the stalk into my mouth. In a single smooth motion, I ingested the stem down to my fingers. That's the point where it gets tough and stringy, so I dropped the stub on my plate and moved on to the next piece.

When I get rolling, I can clean up a pound of good asparagus in no time at all.

There are some foods that are really best when chopped finely. By that time, I had many years of practice using my front teeth for that. I had mastered the art of mincing, biting just hard enough to get the job done but not so hard that my teeth chattered. My teeth moved fast enough that nothing but the smallest bits made it into my mouth. In that fashion, I'd convert a long stringy food like asparagus to something with the consistency of creamed corn.

I made it through eight or ten pieces before glancing at my date. She was looking at me with an expression of such horror that I quickly spit out the last unchewed bite. Had I just eaten a bug or a worm? If so, I couldn't taste it, and the uneaten asparagus looked perfectly fine. But no, the problem was something else entirely.

"We don't eat asparagus with our fingers! If my mother saw you, she would go ballistic." Luckily, Amy's mother was far away. But the way Amy looked, I was unable to continue eating. It was obvious that I had committed a serious food-ingestion blunder, and I was horribly ashamed and embarrassed.

Some guys would have tried to bluff their way out of the situation: "Everyone in Flat Rock eats asparagus with their fingers." However, I knew better. With a sick feeling, I realized I had committed a major social faux pas that any well-domesticated child should have been trained to avoid. I was now an adult. Sophisticated grown-ups were not supposed to make mistakes like that.

But what, exactly, was my mistake?

I had developed particular food-eating rituals that gave me comfort. I separated everything on my plate so different dishes didn't touch; I ate foods in order of best to worst; and I minced my vegetables. By adulthood my system of mincing asparagus was firmly embedded in my psyche. None of the people in my life had ever paid any attention to it, so I'd come to assume it was a harmless and comforting behavior. That night, when I saw Amy's reaction, I saw how wrong I was. It was awful. I was totally humiliated.

That is one of the big problems with rituals, and it's a reason to be really careful with them as you get older. You can find something comforting, and it makes you feel good—until the moment you realize how the rest of the world sees it. At that moment, you realize you look like some kind of freak; your security falls apart and you are left with nothing but embarrassment.

There are other issues with rituals when it's time to get a job. That's when you are expected to conform to other people's nutty ideas and processes, or else you get fired. It's not an Asperger thing at all. It's what people call "corporate behavior," something immeasurably worse. I learned this when I took my first real job, at Milton Bradley, and they handed me a thing called the employee handbook. What I found inside was nothing more than a bizarre set of rituals, each backed up with a threat. *Do this, in exactly this way, or get dismissed!* Strange as my rituals were, theirs were worse. But they were the bosses, so their rituals mattered and mine didn't.

I still find it's easy to get into ritualized behavior. For me, it often seems easier and safer to repeat something I'm comfortable doing than to try new things. That's how I end up doing the same stuff over and over again. Most things I do are totally innocuous, like going to the gym and walking on one particular treadmill in the same program every visit. But I just never know how others will perceive my nonstandard but innocent actions. As the asparagus experience showed, I can never tell when some long-invisible ritual will rise up to bite me just when I least expect it.

I have learned to be wary of my ritualized behaviors.

It's funny that I have learned to be wary of my ritualized behaviors while I've observed that nypicals do many of the same things, yet they just laugh and call them habits. Which is it? Habit or ritual? There are days when I feel like I started life marginalized and I'll never escape that trap. Nypical behavior is the subject of innocent joking, while mine is discussed by serious-looking psychologists with long-stemmed pipes.

So what do I do about it?

I try to pay attention to what I do and watch how people perceive it. I'm really sensitive to stares, snickers, and snide remarks. I've learned to break up and vary my routines, and it's made life much better for me. Instead of ordering an iced tea every day, I sometimes order a soda or sparkling water. But not too often . . . I've decided some rituals, like ordering iced tea most of the time, are harmless, and I'm content to leave them alone.

Here's a good rule of thumb: Your own rituals are okay as long as they don't interfere with your responsibilities in daily life, or make you the subject of teasing or ridicule. Rituals become a problem whenever they prevent you from doing the stuff you're supposed to do, or when they get you in trouble. And it's not a two-way street, because certain of other people's rituals—often called laws—must be acknowledged and obeyed, or else.

> *Your own rituals are okay as long as they don't interfere with your responsibilities.*

If you're lucky, you'll figure that out early and with minimal embarrassment.

What's in a Name?

For as long as I can remember, people have commented on my strange names for things. Like Varmint, my little brother. Or Bugle, the beagle dog. Or Small Animal, our cat. Well, those names aren't strange to me. My names are all based on logic, reason, and knowledge. It's not my fault if others can't follow my thinking.

I have always named the people and pets in my life.

> *For as long as I can remember, people have commented on my strange names for things.*

Perhaps it began as one way a powerless toddler could exert a measure of control over his environment. My mom said, "This is Clarence, our new dog," and I said, "Hi, Poodle," from that moment on. Maybe my choice of Poodle as a name meant more to me than the abstract Clarence. Or perhaps it's some mechanism I don't understand. Whatever it is, it's pretty widespread. Many people—kids and adults—share my naming habit. For example, my friend Bob Jeffway does this, too. He renamed all our colleagues when we worked at Milton Bradley. We ended up with a mix of names, his and mine. Our names became part of the flow of our conversation, totally supplanting the names our colleagues had arrived with. We used his names with total ease and comfort.

"Where's Mister Chips?"

"He's in a meeting with The Snout and Johnson Omni."

In a sense, the names became a sub-language, shared by a few geek engineers. For Bob and me, naming started in childhood and it continues today. But it's unpredictable; not everyone gets a name, and name choices can vary widely. One person will always be George, while another is forever The Plankster. In addition to many people, I sometimes name things and parts of things.

Hind legs are a good example. "People do not have hind legs!" My fourth-grade teacher was very firm on that matter. But she was wrong, I explained. People do have hind legs. We walk on them! Dogs walk on all four legs, and we're more evolved than dogs, so we walk on hind legs alone. But we still have four. We just call them something different. We call our forelegs "arms."

And then there are the things at the end of the legs. "Paws" is a universal descriptor for them. Every four-legged animal I know has something you can rightly call a paw at the end of each leg. It's only us humans that call the things at the ends of our forelegs "hands." Well, maybe us and some chimps, too. Actually, we don't know what chimps call anything, because we can't speak their language. It's just us calling the things at the end of chimp forelegs hands. It's actually kind of presumptuous, if you ask me. When I was a kid, though, no one asked me. They just told me I was wrong. Well, I wasn't. Just because some people call the things at the end of our forelegs/arms hands does not make "paws" a wrong term. It's just different.

That was a very frustrating situation for me. I knew I was right, but my teacher persisted in claiming I was wrong. And everyone knows the teacher always wins. Even when she is shockingly, obviously, horribly wrong.

I used to think "fur" was another troublesome word, one where my usage was right and all my teachers were wrong. "Scratch my fur," I'd say when I wanted to get my head scratched. I assumed fur was the hairy stuff covering all mammals to a greater or lesser extent.

However, I subsequently learned that I was wrong. All mammals have hair, but they don't all have fur. When the hair grows in a mix of short, medium, and long fibers for the purpose of providing better insulation or weatherproofing, we call that multilayered hair fur. When hair grows in one length until shearing—like it does on humans or poodles—we call it hair. And when it emerges in oily, curly form from sheep, we call it wool. That, in a nutshell, is why mink coats, wigs, and sweaters look different. They are all made of hair, but they are not the same as my hair, though they may be similar to yours.

Today, I can admit to that innocent oversight or misinterpretation without shame. Humans do not have fur.

But dogs have hair. However, I've been calling the stuff on my head fur for so long that I'm not about to change now, even if it is technically incorrect. So fur it stays.

Sometimes I surprise people with the names I give places, too. The Repair Center is a good example. We have one here in our town. The sign on the door says, UNIVERSITY HEALTH SERVICES. Some people call it that. They say, "I have a cold. I'm going to head over to Health Services and get something for it."

To me, that whole passage is nonsensical. First, they are not heading over there to get something *for* the cold. They are heading over there to get something to *do away* with the cold. Their goal for the cold is not betterment, as "get something" implies. It's eradication. Elimination. Extermination. Why don't they come out and say so?

Second, the idea of going to anything called Health Services sounds funny. The term doesn't describe what the place does. I'll bet fewer than one percent of the people who walk into that place do so in search of health service. The other ninety-nine percent are seeking repair. Cure of disease. Stitching of wounds. Setting of broken limbs. Removal of warts. To me, those are all repair operations. That's why my name for the place makes perfect sense. It is a Repair Center.

I knew that from the moment I first walked though the doorway many years ago. Why can't other people see it that way? Instead, nypicals often choose an arbitrary or incomplete name for the Repair Center. They say something like "doctor's office." It is a mystery to me how anyone could look at a three-story structure that obviously houses a few hundred people and call it a mere doctor's office. After all, the word "office" usually refers to a single room. At best, it's a small structure containing a few rooms, one of which is the office proper.

I could understand if outsiders said, "I need to visit my doctor. His office is in the Health Services Building." That would be correct, but no one seems to say that. I wonder why.

And then there are the names I give other people. When my newborn brother came home from the hospital, I watched him really closely and listened to him. I was eight years old, but when looking at my new brother, I remembered myself at an earlier age. I wondered what he would do, and what uses I might find for him as he got bigger. My mother told me his name was Chris, but I said that to him repeatedly and he never responded. He just kind of gazed with a blank expression.

My dog knew his name. I'd say, "Hey, Dog," and he'd look up at me. Dog was a perfectly sensible name, because he *was* a dog. I always knew he recognized his name, since he wagged his tail whenever I said it. And sometimes, he barked. My little brother didn't do any of those things. I could say "Chris" or anything else all day long and he just lay there and made little snorts.

So that's what I named him. Snort. My mother objected right away, but I could not see why. My name was just as good as hers. Actually, it made more sense. Anyone could look at my little brother, lying there making noises, and see why I named him as I did. In comparison, there was absolutely no visible reason that my mother had named him Chris. He wasn't like a car, where you could read CHEVROLET or TOYOTA across his forehead and know what kind of kid he was.

It didn't take too long for my brother to begin answering to Snort. Just as the dog would wag his tail when I called his name, Snort would look at me and make faces. I could tell he recognized his name, no matter what my parents said. When he got a little older and became self-propelled, he even came when I called him and followed me through the house. Just like Dog, but less obedient.

However, as Snort got bigger, problems emerged that rendered his name inappropriate. Most significantly, he stopped snorting when he learned to talk. So the previous relevance of his name disappeared. My little brother was fun at first, but he became a nuisance. He took my toys and often broke them. He stole my coin collection and spent it on candy. That was why I decided he needed a new name, and the choice was obvious. Once again, I named him based upon his most obvious attribute. He became Varmint. That's what he remained until he was about sixteen. At that time, I realized he was too old and too big to be called Varmint, but I never liked Chris, so I just stopped calling him anything.

Now I just say, "Hey," whenever I need to speak to him, and that's worked fine for the past few decades. When I refer to him in conversation I usually say "my brother," but occasionally I do use the name my mother gave him. Not often, though.

There are many more examples of my naming conventions, which are often at odds with those of nypical society. In every case, though, I maintain that my names have a sound logical foundation and people are irrational to criticize them.

> *I maintain that my names have a sound logical foundation.*

I've found that people often have problems being named in relation to an employer or a place. For example, I call the people who live in Ludlow Ludlovians, which is entirely appropriate. Yet some Ludlovians object. Why? I didn't put them there. If they don't like being Ludlovian they should move to a place they can be proud of. Don't blame me! The fact is, every town has its denizens. And a smart person knows what they are called. In the English language, "-ite" or "-ian" is added to where you live. It's a language rule, so if you don't like it, move!

Long ago, I worked with people from the Xerox Corporation. They were Xeroids. Today, people who work at Crown Publishing are Crownites, and those at Penguin are Penguites. People who live in Longmeadow are Longmeadeans. A few miles away, Conway has Conwites.

I'm not the only person to approach naming people in this way. Consider all the *Star Trek* fans who proudly call themselves Trekkies. They did that to themselves. I hear a lot of them have Asperger's, so maybe that explains it.

Sometimes my use of strange-sounding names is totally unconscious. It's hard for me to regulate that. Other times, when I am with strangers, I am able to pay attention to my word choices and not call people by names or descriptors they don't expect. That has improved my social success, but it adds one more bit of stress to an already difficult situation.

As a grown-up, I have actually stopped giving names to people, except for those closest to me. Cubby, my son, will always be Cubby, not Jack, but George Parks will always be George, not Woodchuck, as he might have been thirty years ago. The only exception to that rule is when people name themselves. For example, my friend Moira Murphy joined Twitter. When she did, she sent me and all her other friends her new handle, and it started me thinking. . . .

From that moment on, she became and will always remain: Murph Smurf.

Mind Your Manners

When I was younger, people often accused me of weird expressions and strange behavior. As a kid, I used to feel really bad about that, because I was just being myself. I didn't know what I was doing wrong.

Now I see things in a different light. I've learned that other people have certain expectations for how I should look and act. If I don't meet their expectations, especially during a first impression, they won't be friends with me, work with me, or even answer my questions. The onus is on me to act as expected and make a good impression.

To accomplish that, I needed to learn exactly what was expected, how to act "normal" in the situations in which I found myself. The

> *To many people, normal means "well-mannered."*

first step was to figure out what "normal" really meant. To my surprise, the answer to that turned out to be simple: To many people, normal means "well-mannered."

Manners were always something I lacked, according to everyone involved in raising me. I can still remember my mother turning to me when I had food on my face and saying, "Look at you! What would your grandmother say?" She meant to admonish me, but comments like that never worked. I don't think I even grasped the idea that I had food all over me, much less that anyone else could care. With no understanding of those basics, how could I possibly make sense of what she said?

Yet I heard her, and at some level, at that early age, I knew there was a problem. *But what?*

My grandmother Carolyn always complained about my manners. She tried to improve them whenever I stayed with her in Lawrenceville, down in Georgia, but I wasn't very trainable. I found her instructions arbitrary at the time, and I've always been resistant to following orders I felt were foolish.

She was forever comparing me to Leigh and Little Bob, my two first cousins. My cousins said, "Yes, ma'am" and "No, sir" to every grown-up who spoke to them, and she was always pointing out their resultant "good speaking manners" to me. I, on the other hand, tended to ignore or question adult commands that I didn't think made sense. When Little Bob said, "Yes, sir!" and I said, "No!" or "Why?" it never went over too well with grown-ups.

"Why should I talk like that?" I asked my grandmother. "It's a way of showing respect for your elders, son," she said. Carolyn had an answer for everything. But they weren't showing respect, and I knew it. They were just acting, playing a game. As soon as the grown-ups walked away, Little Bob and Leigh made faces at them and laughed at what they said and did. Then when a grown-up reappeared my cousins straightened up and went right back to "Yes, sir!"

I realized they were just like dogs who lay down where you told them when you were looking but, as soon as you turned away, jumped all over the furniture and ate food off the table. It aggravated me to no end when my dogs did that, and Leigh's and Little Bob's fake manners aggravated me, too.

I wanted grown-ups to like me. I wanted to help my family. But I also wanted to play and have fun like kids my age did. And I was truthful. So that made it very hard for me to say, "Yes, ma'am!" when my grandmother asked me to carry the bags in from the car and I was in the middle of solving a complex puzzle. *Couldn't the food wait? My puzzle was far more important!* "No!" I would reply, truthfully.

After enduring years of continued resistance my grandmother eventually gave up on me ever saying "Yes, ma'am," but she never gave up on the rest of manners. As she explained, "The whole thing—manners, behavior, and all . . . it's called etiquette. And that's what you need to get by in life, honey child." She kept repeating that, even after I was fully grown.

Carolyn kept at it long enough that a few things actually stuck. For example, she taught me the right way to hold a knife and fork. Maybe that worked because it made sense. I still don't know of any better or more functional way to do it. Making a fist around the fork—like I did when I was little—is both inefficient and impolite. The polite method of holding a fork provides for better control of the tool. It's a good idea that's also good manners.

(The only time making a fist around the fork helps is when you want to stab someone because he's stealing your food. Now I know stabbing people is really rude, so I hold my fork in the grown-up way all the time, and I rely on discreet snarls to protect my dinner from predators.)

Aspergians like me are notoriously logical and straightforward, and much of the time, manners are neither.

If only all manners were so logical! Unfortunately, they are not. Aspergians like me are notoriously logical and straightforward, and much of the time, manners are neither. They are not "common sense," nor are they "acting right." That's why manners didn't come naturally to me.

Consider, for example, the ingestion of soup from a bowl. When I was small, I used a spoon to eat most of my soup, and then I picked up the bowl, tipped it, and drank the rest. It's obvious to me that the most efficient way to ingest soup is to tip the bowl and drink it. In fact, unless you have a spoon that's specifically contoured for the bowl you're using, that's the only way to get every last drop. And common sense tells us not to be wasteful.

Acting right—the moral imperative to treat others as you'd like to be treated—doesn't say much at all about drinking from the soup bowl. I know it's not right to throw food or jab the person next to me with a fork. But where's the harm to anyone in drinking from a bowl that was given to me by the host or hostess? The answer is, there is no harm.

And yet . . . my grandmother said it's rude to do it. For many years, logic prevented me from complying with rules of etiquette like that. I thought they were illogical and foolish, and I refused to go along. Eventually I came to understand that I benefited from compliance

> *I came to understand that I benefited from compliance with the social rules, even when they seem illogical, wasteful, or nonsensical.*

with the social rules, even when they seem illogical, wasteful, or nonsensical. Today, I look at my bowl, realize that it's better to act polite, and pick up a spoon. In our society of plenty, where I seldom go hungry, a person's positive impression of me is worth more than the small amount of extra soup I'd get by tipping and drinking. I am sure things would be different if I were starving.

And one more thing: I'm glad my family kept up the fight, trying to train me in manners even if it made no sense at all to me. Without their efforts, I'd never have

I'm glad my family kept up the fight, trying to train me in manners even if it made no sense at all to me.

acquired what little manners I have, and I'd have entered the adult world socially handicapped as a result.

That was how I started adult life: with the few manners my family had hammered into me, and whatever innate sense of right and wrong I was born with or was able to evolve. Some people might call that a moral compass, but I wasn't that sophisticated in my terminology. Whatever I called it, it served me well around close friends and family, and it always worked for the big decisions in life. Unfortunately, a logical, morals-based behavioral strategy breaks down in casual interactions, the sort one has at a party.

I learned that as soon as I began venturing out socially as an adult. That's when I encountered strangers who were critical of me and my manners. At first, I reacted with hostility to what I perceived as shallow, superficial posturing. *So what if I don't hold the door for you? Can't each of us take responsibility to open our own doors?* It eventually became clear that logical and ethical behavior just wasn't good enough—I was alienating strangers with my failure to "act like everyone else."

I was nice on the inside, but new acquaintances sometimes never stayed around long enough to notice, because they were aggravated or disturbed by my lack of manners.

"You're acting like a hillbilly, boy," was how my grand-father said it. I never really lived among hillbillies—the closest I came was my grandparents' place in rural Georgia—but I got the idea. If I changed my behavior, people might like me better. I might acquire more friends. It seemed worth a try.

I made that decision in my mid-twenties. That's sooner than some, but later than many. In retrospect, I see that my life would have gone a good bit smoother if I'd made some changes in my teens, and if I'd paid a little more at-tention to those illogical rules of behavior.

Once I resolved to change, the course was clear. I was now an adult. My grandmother had passed away, so there was no one left to train me. I would have to train myself. As I'd done so many times before, I set off for the book-store to look for guidance. I thought manners would be simple, but I was wrong.

The gold standard for manners and etiquette is the Emily Post book *Etiquette*. To my great disgust and amaze-ment, it ran to eight hundred pages! It looked as daunting as the Internal Revenue Code. Still, I bought her book and carried it home.

Emily seemed to have a rule for every possible social situation—thousands and thousands of them. How to act at dinner, at work, in a bar, or at the theater. How to dress, how to walk, and even what to say and when to be quiet. The complexity was just overwhelming. *Does everyone else in the world already know this stuff?* I wondered. Whether they did or not, I quickly realized I needed a simpler system. I remembered what my grandfather used to tell me long ago about watching the older people. Starting with that advice and fortified by snippets of Emily Post, I made my own set of rules. I based my plan on advice from people I trusted, how Emily said I should behave, that moral compass, and a lot of careful observation and contemplation about how I interacted with other people, successfully and otherwise.

> ## I made my own set of rules.

First of all, when in a strange social situation, I watch the others and do as they do. This applies to wearing a suit, handling silverware, eating food, going through doorways, and many other situations. I do a lot better when I watch, wait, and imitate. My grandfather taught me this.

When I speak in casual conversation, I try to start a mental clock in my head. I actually learned this from Marty Nemko, a San Francisco career coach. He told me, "For the first thirty seconds after you start talking, imagine a green light in your head. After thirty seconds the light turns yellow. At sixty seconds, it's red." That's a good piece of advice for most any conversational situation. It takes some mental energy to monitor myself, but it works.

I used to feel that I should say everything as soon as I got a chance to talk, because my contacts with people were so fleeting. After all, I might never get the chance to talk to them again. Today, I realize that my contacts were fleeting because I went on and on, bored people silly, and ran them off. It was a sad day when I finally realized that most people do not care about the 66,000-horsepower MAN B&W diesel engines in the big American President Lines containerships. The world is just filled with important and fascinating facts, yet nypical people just choose to remain indifferent. So I stopped running on at the mouth, or at least I try to.

I've learned to say "please" and "thank you" fairly often. That's a simple rule that delivers good results. I don't always remember to do this, but I know should. There's nothing false or objectionable about "please" and "thanks." Even if I don't like someone, I can thank him for handing me the hammer, and I can say, "Please move over so I can get past you." Those words just make things smoother. People seldom refuse to step aside when asked, and shoving them out of the way without asking almost always leads to a bad outcome, unless you are at a sporting event where manners are not used.

Manners mavens often advise us to go beyond "please" and "thanks," to actually make up nice things about the other person. For example, they suggest things like, "Susan, your dress looks lovely tonight!" I don't usually follow that advice, because I think it results in conversation that's shallow and contrived as people trade fake compliments and false smiles. Some of my relatives act like that, and it aggravates me to no end because I can't ever trust what they are saying. How can I tell if they really mean something, or if they just made it up for the sake of conversation?

Then there's the matter of "polite" clothing. . . .

Nowadays, when I go somewhere, I try to find out how people will be dressed before I go there so that I can put on appropriate clothes. In my antisocial days, dress didn't matter, because I was an outcast everywhere. Now, when I join social groups, I realize it's a lot easier to fit in if I'm dressed in a style that's at least generally compatible with that of the other people. Also, I never go out in public in my underwear.

That simplified code of manners may not seem like much, but it transformed my social life. Today people invite me to events and parties and then invite me back again. Given my social standing in high school, that's something to be proud of. And I accomplish it all with a minimum of posturing and false behavior, and just a little compromise of efficiency.

When I first began studying manners, as a teenager, I assumed they were nothing more than a code of behavior written by and for self-serving adults. From my perspective, therefore, they were pretty much useless. Now, years later, I understand that manners are a code of behavior that makes life smoother and better for all of us. There are times when I am inconvenienced, like when I hold a door for ten people, but at other times I am paid back when strangers do the same for me. I can't always foresee how kindness and consideration will pay off, but they usually do. I believe that because of my manners, strangers observe me and make subconscious decisions to be nice, just as other strangers in earlier years had observed and re-jected me as an ill-mannered child. When I act politely, I build a reserve of goodwill in others. That reserve allows those people to cut me some slack when I do something annoying.

And believe me, I'm no paragon of well-mannered manhood. To be honest, I'm often rude and sloppy. But I am a thousand percent better than I was before I set out to be polite, and the effect it's had on my social life has been phenomenal.

A Reason to Care

By the time I entered high school I was sold on the logical and sensible parts of manners and behavior, but I had some problems accepting why I should do some of the bigger behavioral things, like staying enrolled in school.

In tenth grade I knew kids like me were supposed to graduate from high school and go to college. I loved computers and electronics, so I naturally imagined myself becoming an engineer. Yet even with that dream secured, it was difficult for me to see a clear path from high school through college to professional engineerhood in my head. There were just too many problems. My home life was awful, with a drunken father and a mentally ill mother. And I

> *It was difficult for me to see a clear path from high school through college to professional engineerhood in my head.*

> *I didn't seem to be able to focus on what my teachers wanted.*

didn't seem to be able to focus on what my teachers wanted. Class sucked, so I spent my days in the school Audio Visual Center instead. I even skipped classes to be there. When they threw me out, I hung out downtown. And why shouldn't I? After all, the Hungry U and Augie's Newsstand were far more interesting than the school library. I skipped whole days of school to do that.

When I skipped school, I got a chance to spend more time with the musicians I had started meeting through my budding skill with electronics. Some kids learned to play instruments; I taught myself to fix them. The more of a failure I became in school, the more rewarding that work became.

The problem was partly me and partly the school itself. When I did go to class, I never had it together. I hadn't even begun my homework; and I didn't pay attention on tests. No one from the school ever stepped up to get me back on track, so I continued on a downward spiral. I became a wise guy, constantly in trouble. If I didn't get sent to the office for discipline, I sent myself to the nurse's office for a nap. The result of all that was predictable—a report card of straight Fs. That led to my second year of tenth grade, and the realization that I was not college material.

"You can still graduate," my guidance counselor said.

But I doubted his sincerity as I watched the prospect of graduation, let alone college, receding into the distance. I became convinced high school would never end.

Why bother?

I made a list in my mind. School totally sucked. My first and only girlfriend had just dumped me. I hardly had any other friends. I wasn't getting a thing out of class. No one wanted me there. There was no good reason to be in school. Looking back, I realize that I was very sad at that time, and probably depressed. But I was rational, and I considered my next move carefully.

The world outside was full of opportunity. I was doing more and more work for local musicians, and I could probably join a band full-time. I could probably get work fixing cars, as a mechanic. There were other things I could do, too, like drive a truck or run farm machinery. I was already doing small jobs for people and getting paid. There were days when I had sixty, even ninety dollars in my pocket. When that happened, I felt like a really rich man.

Measured against those tangible prospects, the idea of slogging through high school and then getting accepted at a college and doing it all again for four more years just seemed unreal. The first problem was the humiliation I'd face when every other tenth grader besides me became an eleventh grader. *How many other kids flunked school?* I wondered. I could not imagine three more years of high school.

"Success depends on you," the teachers said. "You have to change your ways. No more cutting classes. And you have to buckle down and do the work." Teachers always said that with a sneer, as if they were taunting me with some unattainable goal.

Today's teachers would have sent me for testing and special-needs evaluation. In 1970, though, that constructive step was some ways into the future. And I have to admit: I looked lazy. I acted surly. I'm sure I played the part of an angry, disaffected, sullen teen perfectly, because I was one. But that wasn't the only reason for my struggle, or my behavior. In fact, it was the behavior that got me through the day.

The thing was, cutting classes and acting up was the only thing that made school bearable. How could I stop? If I'd had the ability to "buckle down" I'd have done it years before. I knew the value of knowledge, but I assumed I could learn anything I needed on my own in the libraries and labs at the university. Besides, I was sure I knew more than enough anyway.

> *If I'd had the ability to "buckle down" I'd have done it years before.*

If I had blown my chance at college, and I could educate myself, why was I staying at Amherst Regional?

"Why should I stay?" I asked my guidance counselor that question over and over. There didn't seem to be an answer. In fact, one particularly worthless guidance counselor said, "Look, if you drop out you are going to end up a loser pumping gas somewhere. Even the Army won't take high school dropouts now!" That did it for me. I could get that kind of criticism at home, for free, from my father anytime. If the best they could do was cheap threats, I was outta there.

I dropped out, or got thrown out, depending on your perspective, at age sixteen. One thing was sure: By the time I left, they didn't want me, and I didn't want them. It was good riddance on both sides.

It felt good to be out of school, though it was also rather scary. People said, "You're an adult now," and I quickly realized what that really meant: *Get a job or starve.* I did whatever I could to make money at first, fixing cars and guitar amplifiers and anything else I could scrounge.

At the same time, I tried to make sense of the grown-up world I now inhabited. Most of the stuff older people suggested or ordered or demanded I do now that I was an "adult" seemed totally foolish and pointless. Good manners. Button-up shirts and clean pants. Brushing and cutting my hair. Cleaning up my language. "How is any of that stuff going to make me happier or better off?" I would ask, but the answers never satisfied me. What's in it for me? No one could ever answer that.

"It's rude to swear in a restaurant," my grandmother said. So what? Why should I care if I'm rude? "You look like a wild man with that hair," she continued. But why should that matter to me? I wasn't looking at me, I didn't have any friends around, and my grandmother liked me no matter how I looked. People's demands were just annoying, and really self-centered. They complained about my behavior because they wanted *me* to change to make *them* feel better. It was all about the other people, not me.

A few years passed, and I established myself in the working world. I made some money, and sustained some damage but came through alive and kicking. Through it all, I remained stubbornly independent. I dressed like I wanted, grew a beard and long hair, and kept pretty much to myself. *Nobody's going to tell me how to dress, talk, and act,* I thought. *And I am going to prove all those people who said I was a loser wrong. Especially my father.*

By the time I turned eighteen, I'd made a name for myself as the electronics wizard for local musicians. I was self-supporting and on my own—I lived with the guys from the band Fat. Social success still eluded me, but my technical abilities helped me make a living and gain some respect in the process. People said I was weird, but when it came to music and electronics, they also said I knew what I was talking about. That's how things stood—right up to the day I met the girl.

That's how things stood—right up to the day I met the girl.

I'd been alone for a good while, since getting dumped in high school. I did my work, rode my motorcycle, ate, and slept. That was pretty much it. Every night I'd sit at my sound board and watch people pair up as my band played; that's what nightclubs were for. Our music set the scene really well for the audience, but somehow what worked for them never worked for me. I wished it would, but it never did. I was beginning to think the bad things people had said about me as a kid might really be true. The demons had followed me out of school and into adulthood. If you wanted to sum me up in two words, these are what they'd be: sad and lonely.

It was in the midst of that sadness that she appeared. I'd seen her a few times before, when we played the Rusty Nail. She was a little shorter than me, pretty, with short brown hair that curled inward at the ends, and dark eyes. I'd come to recognize a lot of girls that came to our shows, but none of them ever paid any attention to me. Until then. This one walked over and talked to me. I was shocked, captivated, and intimidated all at once.

I talked to guys every day. There were the guys in the band, and the guys in the bars and clubs where we played. There were dudes in stores and gas stations and even the cops and bouncers who guarded the door everyplace we played. Somehow, talking to them didn't ease my loneliness. I wanted someone special, someone to really share my life. I wanted a girlfriend.

But as much as I hoped to find love, I had no idea where or how to look. Until suddenly, when she stood in front of me, saying, "That looks really interesting. Can you show me how it works?" She wasn't a girlfriend—not yet—but she was a girl. And she was interested in me. I was so amazed that I can't remember a word of what we said, but I will never forget that first night. Would I ever see her again? I couldn't stop thinking about her on the ride back home, and I thought of her all the next day. And she did return, to sit with me and talk all night.

I watched her closely, and listened to everything she said. She was a nursing student at the university. She was five years older than me, pretty and sophisticated and smart, and to my great amazement, she was remarkably interested in me. How long would it last? I began thinking about what I'd heard. It was time for action.

The next day, I washed all my clothes, even the socks and underwear. I put on my least-perforated blue jeans. I got the scissors from the toolbox and cut my hair. Suddenly, all the things my grandmother had said made sense. I did not want to look like a fright. I did not want to sound like a drunken sailor. I did not want to smell bad. I wanted her to be impressed, and I did everything I could think of to make that happen.

I even polished my motorcycle, in case she wanted to go for a ride. The bike and I were the spiffiest we'd been in years. The guys in the band noticed, and to my surprise they knew just what it meant. "Check it out . . . John has a hot date," they said. I hadn't realized the change would be so obvious, nor had I expected them to divine the reason for it right away. But it was okay. All that mattered was that I looked good for her. I could handle a little teasing from the guys.

It worked. "Would you like to go out after you finish work?" I couldn't believe it—I had just been asked on a date. *That never happened before,* I thought. Was it the clean clothes, or the hair, or something else? I didn't know, and I was afraid to ask. Cathy Moore became the first girlfriend of my adult life. We dined at the Whatley Truck Stop, and then we went for a ride. "Let's go somewhere and look at the stars," she said. We spent the night far out in the country, looking up into the predawn sky. She, me, and my black Honda motorcycle.

I'm sure I was clumsy and a little robotic that first night, and indeed most nights back then. Despite all that or maybe as a result of my inimitable geek charm, things worked out. We held hands and cuddled and talked until the first light of dawn. Whatever she expected of me, I was way too shy and scared to try anything else. After she fell asleep, I lay there thinking, wondering if she would still like me the next day. To my amazement, she did. As the days and weeks passed, we got to know each other better, and I became more confident. She had a car, and we began going places together.

She talked about her own time at St. Brigid's High School in Leominster. Unlike me, she had graduated with honors and then gone on to college. She asked me where I had learned about electronics, and I said UMass, but I changed the subject before I had to admit I was never a real student. I began to wish I had stayed in school. I was starting to feel that dropout stigma. I never admitted leaving school to anyone in those years, but I knew, and it ate away at me.

Now that I had a girlfriend, I began to understand that my behavior and appearance did matter to other people. I hadn't really grasped that before, perhaps because I'd never had a strong enough connection to someone else.

I began to understand that my behavior and appearance did matter to other people.

Now I could see it, and I really did my best, but I was hampered by a lifetime as a feral child. My parents had not done much to socialize me, since they were wrapped up in their own problems, and I had rejected whatever advice others had offered. My problems were compounded by Aspergian oblivion, though I didn't know that at the time. I did my best, but I wished I'd paid attention and gotten an earlier start.

I was almost nineteen years old. I'd left my family, dropped out of school, and joined a band. I'd lived my whole life with little to no regard for what anyone else thought or said. All of a sudden, my world had changed. I had an answer to that cynical question I'd been asking all those years: Why bother? I bothered because I'd learned that having someone to love and cherish was the most important thing in the world to me, and I had to look and act and feel like I was someone she would want to love and cherish back. That was why I had to bother, as much trouble as it seemed.

Years later, Cathy is long gone from my life, married to someone else; but the feeling she brought has never left me.

What Are You Afraid Of?

When I was little we lived in Philadelphia, where the museum was one of my favorite places. Trains and dinosaurs were two of my special interests, and they had both at the Franklin Institute. They had a huge model train layout and several real steam locomotives. They even allowed kids to go up in the cab and work the levers, just like real train engineers. Another room was full of dinosaurs, or dinosaur skeletons. I really liked to wander through the big dinosaur room, but it was different from the train room. With the dinosaurs, I had to be brave, especially when I looked at the teeth on some of those monsters. One of the skeletons they had on display was a plesiosaur, a gigantic meat-eating aquatic dinosaur. "They were fierce," the museum guides said, "but they've been extinct sixty million years. There's nothing to be afraid of here."

I heard his explanation, but I wasn't fooled. I knew that scientists weren't always right when they claimed something was extinct. Take the coelacanths; they were supposed to have been extinct for millions of years, too, but a fisherman caught one off the coast of Africa a few years before I was born. The books I read said that most of the deep ocean was unexplored and unknown—we knew only 10 percent of what lived there. To me, it was obvious that there could be living dinosaurs in the deep sea. There might still be plesiosaurs.

That's the problem with being what grown-ups call a "bright kid." You learn stuff, and some of it is scary. And no one understands why you're frightened.

When my family went to the beach at Atlantic City, in New Jersey, I was brave and went in the ocean anyway, because there were a lot of people there and my parents assured me no one got attacked by dinosaurs. But I stayed in shallow water where plesiosaurs and other aquatic monsters could never get me.

Shallow water also kept me safe from undertows, riptides, killer seaweed, and all the other stuff that lurked at the deep water's edge.

Even with that knowledge I never had bad dinosaur dreams until I read about the Loch Ness Monster. That story got me really worried. I saw pictures of something big swimming in Loch Ness, which was someplace in Scotland. It looked a lot like the plesiosaur from the museum. And it was alive. *Could one appear here? Or up the road at Lake Wyola?*

Sometimes in my dreams a plesiosaur stuck its head in my bedroom window, ready to eat me. *But they live in water,* I told myself. *They can't be in our backyard.* Could I be sure?

"There are no monsters out there. It's okay." My mother would reassure me when I woke up from the bad dream, and eventually I'd fall asleep. But I did worry, and with good reason.

My father was a philosopher, and I tried to tackle the problem the way he did in his classes, by asking myself questions.

People like my mom didn't believe in monsters, because they'd never seen one. With no evidence, why should an ignorant person believe? Mom wasn't a scientific thinker like me. She was just a mom, trying to quiet me down. Any kids who had seen a monster got eaten, so they weren't around to tell the tale. Kids vanished every now and then, and monsters might well be the cause.

What's the downside to a belief in monsters? If they are real and you believe, you are wary and therefore less likely to get eaten. If they aren't real and you believe, you waste time being afraid of an imaginary threat. On the other hand, if they are real and you don't believe, you could come to a really bad end. So the risk of not believing monsters are real is huge, whereas the risk of believing when they're not is minimal.

> *After long and careful reflection, I concluded that monsters may be real and I was wise to be wary.*

After long and careful reflection, I concluded that monsters may be real and I was wise to be wary.

My father liked that. "A famous scientist used that same argument as a reason to believe in God."

Faced with a world of threats, what is a tyke to do? I pondered that question long and hard. I kept my window shut at night so dinosaurs and monsters couldn't smell me or find a way in to get me. It got hot sometimes, but the safety was worth the discomfort. I read about kids who vanished and the only clue was an open window. *Nessie?*

With my window safely closed, my second line of defense was the bed. Before getting in, I always checked underneath to make sure nothing was hiding down there. Then I made sure my toes were always covered, because you never knew what might grab them if they were exposed in the dark. My head stuck out, but there was nothing I could do about that because I knew I'd suffocate if I buried my head in the blankets. *Sometimes,* I figured, *you just have to take a chance.*

I knew some kids covered their heads, but that was really dangerous. We breathe oxygen, but air contains a bunch of other gases besides the oxygen we need. That's why people say things like, "Give me some fresh air." They want air that is full of oxygen, not recycled air that other people have already breathed, where the oxygen is all used up.

That's the problem with burying yourself alive in blankets. You have stale breathed air on the inside and fresh life-giving air on the outside. So covering my head might well be a form of suicide, where I just passed out and died from lack of oxygen. According to my mother, that's what happened when you put a plastic bag on your head. She warned me about that, lots of times. I didn't want to die, so I didn't cover my head with plastic bags or blankets. But I did cover every other part of my body with a blanket, and did everything else I could think of to protect myself from something that would sneak into my room late at night and eat me.

And dinosaurs weren't the only things I decided to be leery of. Everywhere I looked, there were threats. The kids around me were unpredictable. Teachers were just waiting to pounce on me, and punish me for fun. Strangers were worse—they lurked outside the school, waiting to kidnap unwary kids. Whom could I trust? It seemed like my parents were safe, and maybe a few kids, but that was about it.

With all that, you might think I was a scared little kid, but I really wasn't. I was just cautious. Cautious and wary. And prepared.

I don't fear monsters anymore. Even if Nessie is real, she's not going to get me in Amherst, Massachusetts, ninety miles from the ocean. Yet my fear of covering my head with blankets seemed so rational and sensible that I carried it into adulthood. I actually stopped thinking of my wariness to put my head under the covers as a fear. It was like jumping off a bridge—something you just don't do.

> *You might think I was a scared little kid, but I really wasn't. I was just cautious. Cautious and wary. And prepared.*

I was firm in that belief until I got into an innocent conversation with my friend Diane. We were talking about wintertime when she said, "I like to get completely under the covers where it's nice and warm. I pull the blankets right over my head!" I was shocked to hear that. Maybe an ignorant child would do such a thing, but her? Even as an adult, I am always aware of the dangers of insufficient oxygen. I looked at her as she uttered that amazing and reckless statement. *She doesn't look brain damaged. . . .*

I broached the subject gently. "Aren't you afraid of suffocating with a blanket on your head?" She looked at me like I was nuts. "No," she said, in that firm voice teenagers use when addressing total fools.

"Aren't you worried that there won't be enough fresh air under the blanket?" I persisted even though her obvious dismissal of my idea made me think there just might be a flaw in my reasoning. *She is a grown-up, after all, so it didn't kill her. And she raised three kids that I know of, and none of them suffocated . . . or did they? Maybe she started with five and these three are all that's left. . . .*

When Diane challenged me, self-doubt arrived like a bolt out of the blue. I had not thought about heads and blankets in years—I just didn't do it—but I began thinking about it then, quickly and quietly.

Have I ever heard of anyone suffocating under a blanket? I've never heard of one, but maybe they call it crib death or something innocuous. How well do the gases in the air mix through a blanket? I don't know. The warmer it is under the blanket, the less the air is diffusing through the covers, and the more dangerous it must be. A blanket over the head is surely different from a plastic bag over the head. Yes . . .

I decided to be cautious. "I don't know how safe hiding your head under a blanket is. There's more than the risk of suffocation. If the house caught fire you might not see or smell it until too late—" I began elaborating my reasons, but she interrupted me. "You have a lot of irrational fears," she said. I immediately thought of my fear of heights and edges. *Were my fears really irrational?* I was shocked, because her comment wasn't nasty or condescending. It was just matter-of-fact. She was suggesting that the irrationality of my fears must be obvious to everyone. *Could that be true?*

Diane's view was clear, but I wasn't convinced. I've always been a firm believer in that old adage Just because you're paranoid doesn't mean they aren't out to get you. To me, my fears were well thought through and reasonable.

I took a moment to ponder my fear of edges. I am wary of getting too close to the edge when I'm on top of a building or at a cliff side while hiking. Edges can crumble, and I don't want to be standing on them when they do. If you doubt that for a moment, ask yourself where the talus pile at the base of any cliff comes from. The dictionary definition says it all: "A talus is a sloping mass of rocky fragments that has fallen from a cliff." And when it comes to tall buildings . . . they may not crumble, but microbursts and strong air currents are ever-present dangers. The same air currents that launch a hang glider could launch me, if they came at the wrong moment.

"I don't think my fear of edges is irrational," I began,

but I guess she could hear the hesitation in my voice. "Okay," she said, "the edge *can* crumble and wind *can* sweep you off, but the chance of that is so remote, it's still irrational."

All I could think of was, *Not to me, it's not.* I reminded her that hikers found bodies at the base of the cliffs at Mount Tom—a popular local hiking spot—with some regularity. They had to get there somehow. Either the edge crumbled, or winds came, or the people just got dizzy. Or maybe they got pushed. However it happened, if they had stayed a little farther from the edge, most of them would still be alive today.

And I wasn't ready to give up on putting my head under the blanket, either. "Maybe you have been fine under light blankets," I conceded. The emphasis was on the "have been." "But with heavier blankets there's got to come a point where you suffer lack of oxygen." Visions of people swaddled in those heavy felt mats movers use flitted through my mind. She didn't say much, but I could see she remained unconvinced. I am sure she will continue to put her head under the blanket in the future, and I just hope she survives undamaged.

So that's where we left it. Diane thinks I have irrational fears. I think I am reasonably well read, logical, and cautious.

All my friends agree about this: If they had to be marooned somewhere—in the woods or on a mountain— I'd be a top choice to accompany them. Because I am always prepared, and I think of all the risks.

Part 2

Emotions

One of the most important keys to getting along in society is the ability to read the nonverbal signals from the people around us . . . interpreting other people's body language, discerning their facial expressions, recognizing angry or eager or anxious or loving gazes.

I always knew spoken words meant something, and I always heard what people said. My hearing was excellent. But I also figured out early on that words alone often failed to tell the whole story in social situations. As a teenager, I knew I was missing something important, but what was it?

Figuring out what you don't know is very difficult. That's particularly true if you grow up like me—with both me and those around me unaware that I perceived the world differently from everyone else.

Follow me through these stories as I begin to find out what I was missing.

(Not) Reading People

W hen I was a toddler in my mother's family home in Cairo, Georgia, my grandmother would pick me up and make faces at me. I didn't know that lots of grown-ups do that to babies. How could I? One of the fundamental limitations of babyhood is that you have no life experience with which to put other people's actions into context. So I wasn't sure what to make of her when she picked me up and stuck her face close to mine. Mostly, she seemed monstrous and large. The faces she made were like a circus clown's—all exaggerated and weird. I stared back, more puzzled and worried with each strange face she made. Was it funny? Was it dangerous? I could never tell. Finally, she'd had enough. "Why won't you smile at me? You're just a mean little boy!" And with that, my grandma Richter plopped me down on my stubby feet and marched away on her own stumpy legs.

I was not able to fully grasp what had just happened, but

I got the message that she didn't like me very much. I sat back down and returned to my blocks. A little bit sad. A little bit puzzled. Eager to return to the comfort of my imaginary wooden-block world where strange and scary grown-ups did not suddenly appear out of nowhere to pick me up and menace me.

As I got older, I encountered a steady stream of people who'd make "faces" at me and expect some kind of response. People would approach me with big smiles and a hand held out. Who were they? What did they want? They often looked offended when I just stared, and things really got strange if I turned and ran. Other times, people pretended to be crying. They often made

> *I was not able to fully grasp what had just happened, but I got the message that she didn't like me very much.*

snuffling noises, too. Were they hoping I'd give them candy or something to drink out of sympathy? Were they really upset, or just pretending? A crying kid with a bloody knee made sense. A crying grown-up with no visible damage, who knew what that meant?

I never knew what to make of people like that, so I just stared. And it almost always ended badly, with accusations like "What's the matter with you?" or "Don't you care?" How could I care? I had no idea what was going on!

I could never discern anything the matter with me. In fact, I never started those exchanges. It was always other people who approached me and made strange faces or gestures, and then criticized me for not doing what they expected. If they planned to criticize me for not responding to them, why didn't they just leave me alone? There I was, minding my own business, and they came and

> *Sometimes I felt like I was in a cage at the zoo, with nasty people jabbing sharp sticks through the bars.*

poked at me and called me names. Sometimes I felt like I was in a cage at the zoo, with nasty people jabbing sharp sticks through the bars.

I didn't figure out why my reactions always seemed to be out of sync with what others expected until I began studying Asperger's and autism later in life.

Then I learned that we have to go way back, to when we were babies, to find the root of the problem. When a mother smiles at her baby, she may not say anything in words, but her expression sends a powerful message. The baby's brain sees the smile, and, without any conscious thought, the baby's brain makes him smile right back. At the same time, his brain tells him to feel happy, because he's smiling.

My nursery school teacher used to say the same thing: "If you make a happy face, you'll feel good. If you make a frown, you'll be sad." To my surprise, it's true. Aspergian or nypical, our emotions can be triggered by physical actions. For those of us with Asperger's, it's getting us to smile or frown in the first place that's the problem.

We see the smile, just like every other kid. After all, there's nothing wrong with my eyes. The difference is, our brains don't respond to a smile the same way as everyone else's. We Aspergians just don't have that instinctive smile-when-smiled-at response. In some of us, it's totally lacking. In others, it works but is somewhat impaired or slow. I am somewhere in the middle of the range. If you persist in making a face at me, I will eventually respond. But it will take me a while. And if your expression is subtle, the way it often is between grown-ups, I may not respond at all.

Because of my smile-reflex weakness, my ability to feel happiness when you look at me is weak, too. That can be both a blessing and a curse, depending on the circumstance.

I've known for a while I was that way, but until lately I had no idea why. Recently, though, scientists have begun to discover fascinating things about the autistic brain, and why it is that some of us lack the smile-when-smiled-at instinct.

Turns out, everyone has brain cells called mirror neurons that "act out" what we see in other people. When we see someone smile or frown, our mirror neurons make a smile or frown in our own brain, and that puts a smile or frown on our face. Seeing it makes us do it and feel it.

Scientists think that cycle is the foundation for empathy—
the ability to put yourself in the other person's shoes and
understand how he feels, instinctually.

It's remarkable that we have brain cells that evolved
specifically for that task, but it's true. And the neurons
don't respond just to sight. Mirror neurons can act out
feelings that come from sounds, smells, and who knows
what else. It's incredibly complex, and it's kind of neat.

People with autism have mirror neurons just like nypicals, but in us it's like the volume is turned down. A big
smile on your face makes a tiny grin on mine. So I respond, but sometimes the response is so small and weak
you can't even see it. Most people with Asperger's seem to
react like me—weakly. Like with everything else, though,
there's a range. Some people are a bit better than I, while
a few are a whole lot worse.

What does having weak
mirror neurons mean for Aspergians long term?

*What does having
weak mirror
neurons mean
for Aspergians
long term?*

I've thought about that
question a whole lot. I think
that it means it's tough for us
to develop a sense of other
people's realitics, to under-
stand that they have their own thoughts and emotions
that are separate from ours. We are not good at putting
ourselves in other people's shoes. We don't even see the
shoes, figuratively speaking.

When I was a toddler, I got sad and happy and frustrated all by myself. I ate something and it tasted good, so I felt happy and content and fed. I fell and hurt my knee, and cried like the world was about to end, especially if I saw a spot of red blood. I grabbed a shiny new toy and played with it, and it made me happy again. I got stuck in my high chair, and I became frustrated beyond belief as the world passed me by, and I yelled as loudly as I could.

All those feelings originated inside me. No one else gave them to me. The saying "Kids are the center of their own universe" is particularly true for those of us with autism or Asperger's. I was the sun, and my parents and teachers and other kids were all planets, revolving around me. As far as I knew, all thoughts and feelings emanated from me. At least they were supposed to.

How could I know otherwise? Kids who are not autistic feel what others feel by simply looking at them. I could not do that, so I lived in an emotional vacuum, a void that was crossed only by the most extreme emotions, like those of an enraged teacher or an angry parent.

I was made painfully aware that other people had ideas that differed from mine every time I got shaken or spanked because a grown-up had a different notion of what I should or shouldn't do, or when people got mad at me because I didn't respond to their funny faces. I always knew that something had gone terribly wrong in those interactions, but I never knew what or why.

All that time, people were trying to share their feelings

with me, but I didn't get their signals. I had no idea. Neither did they.

My inability to read other people's feelings kept me from developing a good sense of "me" and "you," and our relative place in the world. As a toddler, if I could

All that time, people were trying to share their feelings with me, but I didn't get their signals.

not sense your feelings, how could I know you had any? The simple answer is, I couldn't. That caused me no end of trouble with other kids. If I was playing with Lincoln Logs, and you came up and showed me a truck, I'd say, *"No! Lincoln Logs! No trucks!"* I said that because I was thinking about logs and it just didn't occur to me that you might have your own thoughts and want to play with a truck.

When my grandmother picked me up and made faces at me, I didn't get the signals she was sending. After a few tries, she got frustrated and gave up on me. I may not have understood her facial expression, but I got the message right away when she dumped me on the ground and stomped off—*I was a bad kid.* Scenes like that set the stage for a lifetime of poor self-image.

Eventually, I figured out that other people had their own independent thoughts, but the Asperger's still made it hard for me to read them, so I was always a few years behind my peers. Asperger kids today still face that problem, but if grown-ups are aware, they can do a whole lot

> *If grown-ups are aware, they can do a whole lot to help by explaining what the kids are missing.*

to help by explaining what the kids are missing. That's so important—that and not condemning the kids for something they don't even understand.

I explained what others were thinking and feeling to my Aspergian son, and it worked. I wish people had known to do that for me when I was little.

"Don't worry, he doesn't even notice" was a common refrain when people talked behind my back. Well, let me assure you, I may not have been able to read from people's subtle clues their thoughts and feelings, or their expectations of me, but I absolutely noticed when they rejected or disregarded me, and I still do. I may seem robotic and mechanical sometimes, but there is nothing mechanical or cold about my internal feelings. I am just as sensitive as anyone to snide remarks and criticism. I cried inside fifty years ago, and I still do today.

What Is Love?

Today, some researchers wonder if weak mirroring keeps people on the spectrum from forming strong bonds with their parents. I don't think that's true. I'm absolutely positive that I formed a bond with my parents even though I often misunderstood their expressions and their requests of me. If my life is any guide, long experience with someone forms a very good bond even if the mirroring instincts are weak. I can certainly see someone's actions over a period of time, and I will come to care for that person in response to how he or she acts toward me.

However, even if I'm willing to wait patiently for bonds to form, those around me

> *I'm absolutely positive that I formed a bond with my parents even though I often misunderstood their expressions and their requests of me.*

without Asperger's may not be. They are wired to look for signals of affection from me, and when none are forthcoming, they get anxious. It's an automatic and unconscious thing. I hear about that whenever I speak to parent groups.

Parents ask questions like "Why doesn't my son ever say he loves me?" The first time I heard that, I thought back to my childhood and my mother putting me to bed. She'd say, "I love you," and then abandon me to the unseen terrors of my nighttime bedroom. To the toddler-sized me, that phrase didn't have a very good connotation. Grown-ups expected me to figure out the meaning of their words, separate from the actions that inevitably followed. Well, I never did.

That's not to say I didn't love my parents. But what is love? What I felt was not something I could express in words as a little kid. I looked to them for sustenance, protection, and answers to any of life's questions. Like all kids, I was totally dependent on Mom and Dad, and I knew it. I trusted them to take care of me.

Yet I also feared them, especially my father when he flew into drunken rages. I felt many things about my parents at different times, and I guess the sum total was what you call love. For the most part, my relationship with them just rolled and bumped along. They didn't do much to elicit strong positive feelings in me, whereas they did quite a bit to elicit rage and resentment. Was that love, too?

The conclusion was inescapable: Many aspects of love

just are not very nice. With that perspective, it's no surprise I wasn't quick to say, "I love you."

The inability to read the unspoken signals from other people added up to a childhood filled with anxiety. I thought about that when writing this chapter. *Was my experience typical of kids with Asperger's?*

My first thought was, *All kids with Asperger's must be the same way I was.* Luckily, a moment later, I realized that that was just the old problem of not being able to put myself in others' shoes. I reminded myself that I am not the center of the universe. Note to self: Other kids have had different thoughts.

There are some Aspergian kids whose mirror neurons work better than mine. They may have found real comfort with their parents. There are also kids who grew up in safe environments, who never knew the constant anxiety of an alcoholic family. Some unlucky kids grew up in even more violent or dangerous homes than I did, where there was no safe place, no matter where they looked. Asperger's or not, some grew up more anxious than I, others less. Like almost everything else in the world of mental health, there's a continuum. But I

> **When you can't read the unspoken messages of love, all you have to go on are words and observed behaviors.**

think it's fair to say that many Aspergian kids share my anxiety to varying degrees, and it all started with those broken mirror neurons.

When you can't read the unspoken messages of love, all you have to go on are words and observed behaviors. If my life is a guide, those two ways of communicating messages can be sharply at odds with each other, something that paints a disturbing and troubling picture to an Aspergian kid.

Emotional Triggers

What does it mean when someone leans forward with his arms crossed on his chest? Is he happy? Sad? Aggressive? Reassuring? As you already know, I could never tell. Sometimes that ignorance got me into a lot of trouble.

I can still remember breaking a fancy vase that belonged to one of my mother's friends, back when I was four years old. I picked it up because it was pretty and I was curious. I turned it over to see the bottom, and when I did, the top fell right off and shattered on the floor.

Why did that happen? Pretty things aren't supposed to fall apart when you turn them over! I was embarrassed, and scared, and annoyed because the stupid thing broke, and I'd been holding it in my hand. But most of all, I knew I was in trouble. Even at age four, I knew what would happen. I had broken something nice, and a grown-up would yell at me. I'd been through that before. But this time, the grown-ups surprised me. My mother's friend marched up to me, leaned forward, and said, "That's just great! Look what you've done!" She even had a funny-looking smile on her face.

I pondered her words, "That's just great!" I couldn't imagine why breaking the vase would be great, but she was a grown-up and I was just a kid. What did I know? I was just really relieved I wasn't in trouble. I was totally oblivious to her sarcastic tone of voice, or her hostile face, or her angry walk. The whole concept of a sarcastic smile was way over my head. So I did the only thing that made sense with the information I had. I scrunched up my best smiley face and said, "I'm glad you liked it. I can do it again if you want!"

That was totally the wrong thing to say. She went completely wild, berserk, even, and her hostile intent became unmistakable, even to me. I had to hide to survive.

As an adult, I have a blindness to sarcastic tone, body language, and expression.

As an adult, I have the same blindness to sarcastic tone, body language, and expression, but I've concealed it beneath an overlay of life experience. I now know that there is no conceivable reason that I'd be praised for breaking her vase. Today my life experience would tell me that her words were not telling the real story, and I'd be able to respond in a more "normal" way. My first thought would still be, *Who'd have thought the stupid thing would fall apart when I picked it up!* But now I know enough not to say that, even though it's true. Today, I understand that the vase may indeed have had a design defect, but it was my picking it up that tipped the balance. So the only socially acceptable response is to apologize, and I do.

Actually, thanks to life experience, I'd also recognize her response for what it really was—snotty and nasty. That would diminish my desire to apologize, but I'd probably do it anyway because of the little bit I know about manners. According to Emily Post, when you break someone else's stuff, you apologize even if the stuff was poorly made and just waiting to fall apart.

I've learned a lot about reading nonverbal communication since growing up, too. I'd combine that with my knowledge of what it means to break other people's stuff and their spoken words to conclude . . . sarcasm. When I was growing up, I heard that word, and I thought I knew what it meant, but I never recognized sarcasm when I heard it or saw it expressed by other people.

When two people talk, their interaction takes place at several levels. Most of the "conversation" is not even audible. The messages between two people are sent through subtle changes of posture, facial expressions, and gestures. Those unspoken signals can carry almost all of the emotional content of a conversation. They are what set the feelings—warm, anxious, angry, or happy. But until recently, I had no idea there was anything to a conversation but the words themselves.

It's like I am missing half of the conversation, and I always have been. The left side of my brain is running full

> *It's like I am missing half of the conversation, and I always have been.*

speed, analyzing the words I am hearing. I don't have any impairment at all in my ability to make sense of people's speech. It's the other side where I have problems. While the left side of my brain is analyzing the language, the right side is supposed to be listening to the speech the way you'd listen to a song. My right brain hears the tone, the cadence, and the melody, but it doesn't "read" those signs or discern what my partner meant by sending them.

As a kid, I sensed that the emotional content of a conversation was expressed by people's faces, bodies, and tones and that I was pretty weak at interpreting all that. In school, we heard about reading body language, and I just assumed other kids were like me. Looking back, I know that I was different. Nypical kids picked up lots of things I missed.

Now that I'm aware of my natural weakness, it's just one more problem to be solved. By careful study I've learned enough to get by. I may not get it right every time, but I'm proud to say I "get it" more often every day.

Luckily, blindness to other people's unspoken conversations can be compensated for. That's because many, many people—not just Aspergians—suffer from this blindness to some degree. There are plenty of good books on reading body language and on nonverbal communication. I've described a few of them in the appendix (see "Books" under "For Further Study").

Reading about and studying body language and expression have been a big help. But there's still a gap between me and many nypicals because our responses are often very different even when we both understand the same message. An angry person looks at them, and they get angry, too. It's a gut thing, instinctive. An angry person looks at me, and I say to myself, *Hmmmmmm, he looks angry.* It's more of an intellectual process for me. I get the message, but it doesn't necessarily produce a response in me as it would in a nypical. Still, I'm light-years ahead of where I was before, simply because today I continually work to "get it." Thanks to that, I've actually minimized my disability well enough that few people pick up on it at all.

Yet it still hurts when people notice my different behavior, because it tends to happen in a critical context. "You're not paying any attention to me" and "You don't even care" are

> *I've actually minimized my disability well enough that few people pick up on it at all.*

two refrains I've heard all too often. Even today it just crushes me to hear words like that, because they show the huge gap between the feelings inside of me and how the outside world perceives me. I can be crying for someone inside, and he or she thinks I'm laughing or indifferent.

Can my expressions and behavior really be that far from the norm?

From people's reactions to me, I can tell that almost every time someone around me gets a small cut or scrape, I fail to show the proper sympathy. Or when someone gives me something, I say "thank you" politely, but the "grateful smile" is missing.

The worst thing is when I completely miss something because I'm preoccupied and my senses—such as they are—are almost turned off. That's what happened recently when my friend Alan was jumping up and down with excitement, waiting to tell me about his new job, and I said in a flat voice, "Good. Have you got my car keys?" I looked up from my computer screen, and I thought I was paying attention and responding appropriately. After all, he had borrowed my car, and my first thought was to get

I know there is nothing at all wrong with my ability to feel joy or sadness or love or anger or anything else. All that's missing is the trigger.

my keys back. But the moment I saw his face, I realized I'd been totally inconsiderate, and I felt awful. I almost wished I could be a little kid again, before I trained myself to pick up people's expressions. Back then, I was blissfully content, not knowing when I hurt other people's feelings. *Not knowing* . . . those two simple words hold the key. I never fail to care when I know, but all too often, I don't know when I need to care.

In my own defense, I think my life experience shows that I feel things at least as deeply as anyone else. After all, people often say I'm exceptionally kind, sweet, and gentle. Those aren't words you'd say about an inconsiderate beast. I know there is nothing at all wrong with my ability to feel joy or sadness or love or anger or anything else. All that's missing is the trigger. With a nypical person, one look from someone else can set those emotions roiling. With me, it takes more than a glance. But once my emotions get going, they are as strong as anyone's.

Making and Keeping Friends

In high school, I could recognize extremes of emotion. I knew enough to run if a guy came yelling and screaming at me with a baseball bat. But a girl with a subtle expression on her face . . . was she smiling at me? Laughing? Quizzical and curious? I had no idea. That led to a lot of awkward interactions and years of loneliness.

I've worked to adapt as an adult, and though I still don't read expressions well, I'm skilled enough that most people never know I am "socially blind" in that way. What I'm lacking with regards to the nypical gift of reading people instinctually, I compensate for with good observation skills and logical analysis. When I apply my observation, analysis, and past experience to reading people, the result is good enough to get by.

My Aspergian way of seeing people has shaped

> *My Aspergian way of seeing people has shaped how I act when I meet someone.*

how I act when I meet someone. It begins when the person approaches me. With people I know, the starting tone of our interaction depends on how our previous interaction ended, and our shared history. If there was tension when we parted last, I'll approach with caution. If we parted on a happy note, I prepare to start off the same way. When I see you walking toward me, I scan my memory banks to recall what we were talking about, and what the mood was the last time we were together. That's what tells me to act open and friendly, or cautious and reserved. I start out that way, and see if there's a match with your behavior. Most of the time, there is.

There are times, though, when matching the previous mood doesn't work. For example, if we were energized the last time we saw each other, I might say, "Great, you're here! Let's get going!" Previous experience has told me that is the correct behavior with which to continue our dialogue, and you should respond in kind. But let's say you don't. You say, "Dude, back off! I'm having a bad day!" When I was younger, I'd have blamed myself for that failure. Today, if there's a mismatch between us, I know enough to ask if something has changed in the other person's life. I'll just say, "What's wrong?"

Sometimes I hear how my failings distressed the other person, but more often I hear a tale of woe that has nothing to do with me at all. "I got an F in statistics and I'm really bummed and my parents are going to be really upset. . . ."

At that, I'm relieved, and I might even smile. I had

trouble with exchanges like that as a kid because other people thought my smile was meant as an insult. They assumed I was taking pleasure in their misfortune, and that made them angry. "You're *glad* I got an F! Wait till it happens to you, and I'll laugh, too!" It's like I disrespected the person, when I really meant nothing of the sort.

Today I try to quickly set things right. "No, man, you've got it all wrong. I'm sorry you got an F. What I'm smiling about is that you're not mad at me. I was happy to see you, and you looked so angry, I thought I'd done something really bad."

Anyone can understand that explanation. It's obvious once I say it, but before I do, nypicals take my expression the wrong way. It's ironic—I fail to understand the nonverbal cues of nypicals, and they fail to read signals from me. It's as if we are speaking two different languages. The result: a two-way street of failed communication. (It's nice to know the failures aren't all mine.) Naturally, I relate better to familiar people. They know and value me enough to give me a break when there's a bump in the conversational flow.

> *I fail to understand the nonverbal cues of nypicals, and they fail to read signals from me. It's as if we are speaking two different languages.*

I am at my greatest disadvantage when meeting strangers, because with them I don't have any memories to work from. Plus, I can't generalize behaviors or even expressions from one person to another. I can't look at a stranger's face and think, *She's smiling just like Amy. When Amy smiles like that she's happy, so this person is probably happy, too.* Instead, I watch and evaluate, with a slightly anxious feeling. It's as if I have to build a behavior database for every single person I meet in life. When I encounter someone for the first time, the slate is blank and I don't know what to expect.

New acquaintances also need experience with me, to get used to the way I act. Some people accept that I behave differently; others can't. I always feel uncertain when I'm around people I don't know, as I ask myself, *Are they going to think I'm a jerk and reject me?* People who become my friends develop an expectation for what I'll notice or miss.

> *New acquaintances also need experience with me, to get used to the way I act.*

After knowing me awhile, they figure out that I care about them even if I don't smile or frown at their stories. They learn that I show caring in other ways, and that excuses my face's failure to respond to their changing words and expressions. That's really one of the root problems of autism: We care a lot, but all too often our caring is not triggered by the things nypicals respond to, and our caring may manifest itself in strange or unexpected ways. That can cause other people to think

we are cold, aloof, or even sociopathic. That's what people said about me for many years.

When I was young my social failures led me to have low
self-esteem, and I didn't see any reason anyone would want
to be my friend, unless he was also some kind of freak or
reject. Today I know different. I know I have many likable
traits, if only people take the time to discover them. That's
the trick—I have to act in ways that make people hang
around long enough to see my good side. And the same is
true for every other person on the spectrum. Social impairment does not equal unlikable, except in the most superficial sense.

Like anyone, it cuts me when a friend I care about turns
on me, but if someone I just met fades from the scene, I've
learned not to be too troubled. In the first case, the friend's
abandonment of me is a rejection, and no matter what,
that's hurtful. But when a new acquaintance fails to stay
connected, that's not a rejection at all. Rejection implies
previous acceptance, and when you don't connect with a
new person, that acceptance never happened. So it's a simple
failure to connect. I've learned that some people go together and others don't, and it's natural that some of the
folks who meet me won't "fit" well enough to connect.
Now that I understand that, rejection from someone I
don't know is not much different from finding the wrong
plug when you go to make a connection to your computer. It's annoying, but you keep looking for the one that
fits.

Of course, I wish compatibility between two people were as obvious as matching up the cables on a computer. I worried about my own incompatibility a lot when I was young, because I didn't meet many people and I thought I might never make friends. Today, I know there are compatible friends and mates for anyone, if only we can find them. I sure wish I'd known that back in high school.

There was a time when I saw relationships as all-or-nothing. I had a few close friends, and did not care one bit for the rest of humanity. Today I recognize that I can have degrees of friendship and connection with people, which widens my circle considerably. A nice person who's a bit strange can still be an acquaintance, and I can still have enjoyable conversations with him. I may not share my innermost secrets, but that's okay. I've learned that valuable insights can come from the most unexpected people and situations, and I benefit from greater openness.

> *There was a time when I saw relationships as all-or-nothing. . . . Today I recognize that I can have degrees of friendship and connection with people.*

Presumably other people derive the same benefit, because the concept of limited friendship seems to work for many of us. There is a point, though, where I draw a line with new acquaintances. There are certain things people can say from which there is really no turning back.

For example, "I think you're trying to cheat me" or "I think you're lying" is a relationship killer for me. Where do you go when someone says that? If a person believes I cannot be trusted, there is no basis for any further exchange.

I once interpreted statements like that as a response to my gaze or my way of speaking. With a sense of shame I assumed that my own behavior had precipitated that reaction, so it was somehow my fault. Now that I'm older, I understand nasty phrases like that are more often a commentary on the speaker. Life experience has taught me that people who are quick to say, "You're trying to cheat me" are most often cheats themselves. As one of my teachers said, it takes one to know one.

Today, it does not bother me to hear such remarks, because they identify the speaker as a person I do not wish to be associated with. For me, that marks the end, and I move on.

Then there are the folks who say things like, "I don't usually associate with your kind, but I'll make an exception in your case." Once again, those statements are often a reflection on the speaker. Anyone who identifies me as a "certain kind," and then demeans "my kind," should not expect anything from me beyond a boot and the door, even if their words are couched in syrupy fake politeness.

At times like that, I remind myself that friendship works

both ways. Some people will reject me, but there will be others I will reject. It's a two-way street. That's a powerful realization, because I used to think I had to accept everyone. I'm a lot happier now that I know that isn't true. I have the right to choose my friends, and I do.

Feeling Bad News

When I was seventeen, I spent a lot of time at my friend Adam's garage. It was an old carriage house, with a greasy wood floor, out behind his parents' place in Amherst. There were motorcycles and motorcycle parts everywhere you looked, even downstairs under the floor. My own bike sat out front next to Adam's. We were two misfits surrounded by stacks and piles of wonderful machinery.

We'd sit there in the shade and polish our engines with old bits of oily rag and pink Simichrome polish. There were always carburetors to tune, chains to oil, and brakes to adjust. It was a nice, peaceful way to pass the time. Adam even had a few other friends, some of whom would pop in to visit or share the latest tidbits. One day, Adam's friend Charley stopped by with some bad news. "Did you hear about Peter Pepul? He was in a bad crash on his bike last night. He might lose his leg. What if he ends up crippled? It's scary. He's over at Cooley Dickinson Hospital right now. They took him there last night, after the accident."

"Woof. That sucks," I said, as my mind started churning. Both Adam and I were thinking about Peter as Charley continued with his story, but our thoughts couldn't have been more different. Adam was wondering if Peter would recover, while I was thinking about whether I too would lose a leg in a motorcycle crash. *After all, I'm the same age, I also ride a bike, and we have other similarities. Are motorcycle crashes contagious? Would I be crippled? How would I be able to work and support myself? Would I starve, in addition to getting mutilated?* I started feeling more and more worried. I was actually becoming physically uncomfortable. A psychologist might even say I was having a panic attack.

How did Peter's disaster become my disaster? The more I listened, the more I felt like it was me, bound up in a cast, over there in the hospital. Moments before, I had been enjoying a beautiful spring day. Now, it had all gone bad. All I needed was an IV in my arm to complete the nightmare.

In a matter of moments, my friend's accident had turned into a deadly threat hanging over my head. And it was all in my mind.

In a matter of moments, my friend's accident had turned into a deadly threat hanging over my head. And it was all in my mind. Peter had been riding at night, fast, in the rain. I was parked, on a milk crate, in a garage in the daylight. Any reasonable person would say I was perfectly safe. The motorcycles around me weren't even moving. There was absolutely no reason to think I was about to lose my leg in a bike accident. Yet I felt scared and worried. Was I worried for him, or for myself? And why did I feel threatened?

Perhaps the answer lies in empathy: how it works for nypicals, and the way it works for me. For example, I can see a person crying in the street, and feel nothing but puzzlement. But tell me a story of a motorbike crash, and I get all anxious imagining myself in the same situation.

I got a clue to that when Adam's girlfriend, Brya, came out of the house to hear the story. First, Brya expressed sympathy. She said something like, "Oh! That's terrible! I feel so bad for him. Poor Peter!" As she said the words her face contorted into a sort of sad, crying expression. That's the mirroring mechanism I described a few chapters back at work. Charley felt bad, and Brya mirrored his distress. Then it was time to respond. She instantly turned upbeat in her tone and expression.

"I'm sure he will be fine. It's probably not as bad as it looked, and even if it is, they have good doctors over there and he's young and strong. He'll be okay!" And that last was said with a smile, a total transformation from a few moments before. So Charley's bad news was received, acknowledged, and countered with a positive and upbeat prediction. Peter was going to recover.

It was quite a performance! The word "performance" makes Brya's behavior sound made up or insincere. Yet I'm quite sure it wasn't. I've known her for many years and I am convinced her feelings and actions were genuine.

I am fully confident that her words of encouragement were just as real to her as Charley's distress was to him.

The whole exchange played itself out in just a few seconds. Let's recap what happened:

> *Charley looked distressed as he told us about Peter's accident.*
> *Brya mirrored that distress and expressed sympathy.*
> *Brya turned upbeat and offered Charley words of encouragement.*
> *Charley felt a little better and Brya continued on her jolly way.*

My response was totally different. I could never feel or express the range of emotions that flowed between Brya and Charley in that short period. I could say some of the words, but it wouldn't be natural, and her range of expressions was totally beyond me.

Like I said in the beginning, when I heard Charley's news I furrowed my brow and said, "Woof. That sucks." My words summed up the situation nicely, and my serious demeanor was acceptable, even if it wasn't as expressive as Brya's face. However, it didn't sound very sympathetic or comforting to Charley. And that wasn't all. I continued, in a realistic vein. "I'd be worried about his leg, too, with what you said. What would he do if they had to take it off?"

Some people would say I'm a pessimist, always looking for the worst case, but that's not true. I'd say I'm more of a survivor, and my instinct is to anticipate the worst and plan for it. That way, the final outcome is always better than I planned for. Perhaps my brain design makes me that way.

To me, there just wasn't anything to smile about. I knew Peter might well be crippled. His bike was almost certainly a total loss, too. He was in serious trouble over there at the hospital. And to top it off, he might be facing charges from the police for causing a crash. It was one of those

Some people would say I'm a pessimist, always looking for the worst case, but that's not true. I'm more a survivor, and my instinct is to anticipate the worst and plan for it.

stories that just got worse the longer you listened. At least that's how I saw it. A flowchart of my exchange with Charley would look rather different from Brya's:

> Charley looked distressed and told us about Peter's motorcycle crash.
> I mirrored his distress and expressed understanding.
> I agreed Peter was in big trouble.
> Charley felt a little worse, and I felt anxious as I absorbed Charley's distress and made it my own.

Meanwhile, Brya maintained a smiling, upbeat attitude. How could Brya and I possibly see the situation so differently? We both felt bad about Peter's accident. But from that starting point our responses went in totally different directions. Brya's response was more productive, because both she and Charley ended up feeling good at the end. After my exchange, both Charley and I felt worse.

I think the difference was that Brya responded emotionally and I responded logically. Emotion told Brya, *Charley's in pain. Try and say something to make him feel better.*

Logic told me, *Peter's in trouble. I should acknowledge his predicament and plan for the worst case.*

And why did Brya feel okay at the end, while I ended up feeling so bad?

I'll lay that one at the feet of those mirror neurons. They seem to have operated very differently in the two of us. Brya mirrored Charley, saw a response, and made a happy face to cheer him up. Her happy face cheered her up, too, allowing her to recover from mirroring his worry over the accident. So in the space of an instant she mirrored his distress, countered it with a smile, and felt better herself. That's a successful and powerful system. I wish I had access to it.

My mirror neurons moved slower, and maybe deeper and stronger. I frowned as I acknowledged Charley's sad story. I expressed agreement that Peter might be in real trouble. All the while, my mirror neurons were assimilating Charley's news. The more they took it in, the more I mirrored his feelings, and the worse I felt.

Since I have trouble taking in other people's perspectives as separate from me, I began relating this new bad feeling to myself and the world around me. I was mirroring "bike crash" so naturally that my mind turned to my own motorcycle and the imminent prospect of a wreck. Was I going to get run over by a car the moment I left Adam's? My logical mind veered off track into a world of emotion. But it was wrong emotion, just as it was illogical.

It's also possible that autism makes my sense of self weaker than Brya's. Recent neuroscience studies support that idea. The distinction between the concepts of "me" and "you" may be a little more blurred for me at times. As often as I've been criticized for lacking empathy, exchanges like this leave me feeling like I have *more* empathy than nypicals. My feelings of empathy move a lot slower than Brya's, but once they get going, look out! They're very real.

My empathy reaction seems to have been triggered by my absorption of Charley's words. I'm not sure if the same can be said for Brya. I think she picked up Charley's worried facial expression and his body language, and she responded immediately. I totally missed those things, but his words affected me powerfully, albeit a lot more slowly.

Now that I understand that difference, I feel a little better. But there's still not much I could do if the events happened again tomorrow.

And the result is, bad news knocks me down. I get back up, but it takes a while. I wish I could explain how I turned this particular Aspergian trait to my benefit, but I can't. It's a weakness, pure and simple. The best I can hope for is to know it's there, and understand it, and work to minimize its negative impact on myself and those around me.

When I was younger, I used to think words like "empa-

> *Bad news knocks me down. I get back up, but it takes a while.*

thy" were easily defined and their meaning was clear-cut. Today I understand that the ideas are not so simple. My Aspergian brain processes news like Peter's differently than a nypical's brain, and the result is that I feel bad in a totally different way.

Some psychologists would say that whatever that is, it isn't empathy. But I beg to differ. It may not be nypical empathy, but it is one aspect of what empathy is to me. And it's just as real as the feelings imagined by the nypicals who wrote the dictionary definition.

I hope Peter isn't crippled too badly.

No, that's wrong. I'm sure Peter will make a full recovery.

A really speedy recovery.

Hopefully.

Keeping Cool in a Crisis

S o I don't respond the way people expect, and that's put me at a disadvantage more than once. But there are times when my Aspergian logic gives me a leg up on the nypical population. One example would be during an emergency response, like what happens when cars crash and bodies are lying in the road.

If you are going to be helpful in a crisis, technical knowledge isn't always enough. Sometimes you need something else—what some people call a cool head and a strong stomach. That can be extremely valuable when bad things happen.

There are times when my Aspergian logic gives me a leg up on the nypical population.

You read about people getting hurt or killed in car accidents, and it's kind of an abstract thing. It feels very different when it actually happens to you. What you do in the moments after a crash can spell the difference between life and death for someone, and it's in those situations that some Aspergians can really excel.

I got into a bad car accident with my geek friend Jim Boughton when we were both in our early twenties. We were driving over the bridge from Northampton to Hadley on a Tuesday night, when an oncoming car swerved out of its lane, crossed the double lines, bounced off the car in front of us, and rebounded straight into my grille.

Everything happened in slow motion, though the crash played out in a fraction of a second of real time. Jim saw a rainbow as the other car's window glass exploded in our headlights. I remember a tremendous jolt, and struggling to twist my wrecked steering wheel as our car slid to a stop. When we stopped moving we both looked back and forth for a moment, and wiggled our arms and legs to ascertain that we were still alive and intact. I realized my glasses were missing, and Jim reached forward and pulled them from the dash, where they had jammed at the base of the windshield. As I unbuckled my seat belt I saw that it was stretched and the metal was bowed where the shoulder belt exited the door pillar. The brake pedal was pushed right into the floor from the impact, and the steering wheel was bent forward into the dash.

"Good thing we had seat belts," we said together. Amazingly, our doors still opened, and we stepped out into the road. Our car was cracking and ticking as the metal cooled, but it wasn't on fire and seemed stable. We were a little shaky, but we walked all right and gathered speed and functionality as we moved. The destruction became more apparent as we stepped forward. The hood was folded up into the windshield, and everything beneath it was compressed and pushed back several feet. Where had the engine gone? It took a moment to realize it was now jammed under the floor. Clearly, my vehicle was a goner. We walked toward the car that hit us, wondering what we'd find.

The attacking vehicle had been so totally destroyed that I could not even tell what make it was until I walked all around and read SUBARU on the deck lid. We were both stunned from the impact, but we figured the people in the Subaru were probably worse off, so we'd hurried to check on them.

It took just a few seconds to reach the passenger side of the car, and when we did, the rider was obviously beyond help. He had been killed on impact, impaled by torn metal. It was an ugly scene. Blood dripped from the passenger door sill and pooled on the ground beneath the car. The whole right front was sheared off, from the grille to the passenger seat. Shards of glass and torn metal, empty liquor bottles, loose papers, and a bloody college notebook littered the road. The scene was lit with headlamps from the stopped traffic. Their shadows and glare made the scene even more macabre.

We could see right into the car, because there was not a single piece of glass left in place, and what we saw wasn't pretty. There was no one in the driver's seat, but a weak moan led us to the operator, folded into some wreckage where the backseat used to be.

Jim and I pulled as hard as we could to lever the twisted door out of the way, and we bent the seat frame aside to extract the driver. He was somewhat mutilated from shattered glass and steel, but he had all his parts, which was more than could be said for his passenger. We worked fast, because the front of the car was still leaking gasoline and oil onto the road, and we knew it could catch fire at any moment. If it did, the driver would surely die, because he couldn't move on his own.

Some people would be overcome by emotion at a scene like that. The wreckage, the noise, the blood. Not me. I saw a problem to be solved. There was a wrecked car in the road, and a wounded guy trapped inside with a dead guy next to him. It didn't take two seconds to realize there was nothing we could do for the passenger, but the driver was in immediate peril, and we got him out and safe right away.

> *Some people would be overcome by emotion at a scene like that. . . . Not me. I saw a problem to be solved.*

We tied a shirt around his arm to stop the bleeding, and got him seated at the curb fifty feet from the crash. To my disgust, the driver began talking. He started mumbling, "I wasn't driving. I was in the backseat." Over and over, like he was rehearsing the lines he would tell the cops. I could smell the liquor on him from three feet away. I didn't say anything, but I was revolted.

With the driver secured, we both turned to directing traffic around the accident. By the time the police arrived, the situation was under control. One of the cops walked over to the car, encountered the dead passenger, and threw up on the hood. By then the crash scene was full of people, gawking and milling around.

The ambulance arrived and took the driver to the hospital. He was cut up and had a few broken bones, but he made a full recovery. The medics said our home-brew tourniquet saved him from going into shock with his arm sliced open. We got in a wrecker and left with my car on the back. I got another shirt when I got home.

In that situation, my Aspergian nature allowed me to remain calm and unemotional. When I saw blood and wreckage, I did not "see" emotion. Instead, I simply saw problems to be solved and I jumped right in. That was the best possible thing I could have done. Situations like that are best handled by a calm, logical person who keeps his wits about him. Some people would say I was cold and unemotional, but I think

> *My Aspergian nature allowed me to remain calm and unemotional.*

I showed great empathy by taking the steps to get the driver out of danger and to secure the scene. What more could anyone have asked, empathetic or otherwise?

I helped because it felt like the right thing to do. The

people in the Subaru had hit me and ruined my car; they were totally at fault and drunk to boot. However, I put that concern aside, because I immediately realized that their lives were more important than my car. I didn't ask anything of the person at the scene, and I willingly and immediately placed myself at risk to save him. I didn't have to do that; neither did Jim. What would you call that if not real empathy?

I've often thought that Asperger people may be well suited to work as emergency responders for that reason. We may seem gruff and even uncaring, but our logical minds see the problems and the solutions fast, and our lack of emotional sensitivity protects us from the horrors of car crashes and fires. Asperger people can do well as military medics or emergency room doctors for the same reason. Those are a few examples of important careers people like me are suited for by virtue of a trait that's regarded as disabling much of the time.

Part 3

Getting Along
with Others

Getting along with other people has always been a challenge for me. When I was little, the challenge was learning to play without ending up in a fight. That was tough, because I was sure the other kids played wrong and I knew all the answers.

When I got older, the challenge was in making friends. That became critical in my teen years, when I wanted a girlfriend more than anything else, but I just could not overcome my shyness, social ineptitude, and fear.

Challenges continued when I became an adult and I learned that no one hires a jerk. People have to like me well enough to let me into their circle, whether that circle is a job, or a club, or any other group in which other humans gather.

As an adult, I've finally learned to make and keep the friendships that sustain me, in a reasonable state of middle-aged contentment. In these next chapters I talk about some of the ways I've moved toward that great goal of lasting friendship and social success.

The Center of the Universe

When you walk into a room and change the channel on the television without asking, you can bet that whoever was there before you will have something to say about it. "Hey, what about me! I was watching that!" I've heard complaints like that more often than I can count: first from my parents, then from my little brother, and finally from my friends, and even strangers at parties. I haven't been able to change my ways, though. When I walk into a room, if the "wrong" show is playing, I change the channel.

Usually, I'm so focused that I don't even notice someone else is in the room. What could I be so focused on as I walk to the television? you might ask. All I can say is, I'm lost in my own thoughts, as I usually am. I can walk into a room, look a person straight in the face, and change the channel. It's like I don't even see him. Traffic cops say, "Ignorance of the law is no excuse," when writing tickets, and that's true. But all too often, I am ignorant of how my actions affect other people, and in this situation, I am often even oblivious

All too often, I am ignorant of how my actions affect other people.

of them. That's gotten me in lots of trouble over the years, and has made it very difficult to make friends.

(There's also the issue of what's being watched. I've always had a lot of trouble understanding who in his right mind would want to watch the shopping channel when there's a show about trains, the Alaska pipeline, or the Port of Los Angeles on. The way I see it, I am doing those people a favor by introducing them to something that's really educational and worth watching.)

I don't think altercations over the television make me a bad person, but people tend to interpret my actions as egocentric or self-centered. Can that really be what I'm like? At first I didn't think so. But the more I was called self-centered, the more I began to worry.

I listed the most common complaints I heard from others:

> *"Didn't you give any thought to how someone else might see this?"*
> *"Did it ever occur to you that I was using that when you took it?"*
> *"Do you ever consider the other person's feelings?"*

Accusatory questions like those told me that people found me terribly inconsiderate, to say the least. I knew I wasn't trying to be. I was surprised to learn, however, that people seemed to think that I had a duty or an obligation to consider their feelings before I did something. *Could that be true?* But every person thinks of himself first, so everyone is self-centered to a degree. That's why people get annoyed. I get in *their* space or interfere with *their* idea of how an interaction should play out.

At first, the knowledge that everyone is self-centered led me to dismiss the allegations against me. But the more I learned about myself and Asperger's, the clearer it became that self-centeredness was not the problem; it was merely the symptom.

> *But the more I learned about myself and Asperger's, the clearer it became that self-centeredness was not the problem; it was merely the symptom.*

I decided to learn more about what being self-centered means to nypicals. With that knowledge I could examine my own behavior and consider my next move.

I asked several of my nypical friends what being self-centered meant, and they all said essentially the same thing: A self-centered person is someone who gets ahead at the expense of others.

When I heard that, I challenged my friends. "Do I seem to get ahead at other people's expense?" All my friends agreed—I didn't do that.

Their answer highlighted an important point. Self-centeredness means something different for Aspergians and nypicals. Self-centered nypicals are fully aware of others. They have their plans and goals, and they seek to exploit those around them for their own gain. If someone did that to me, I'd be annoyed, too.

That runs totally counter to the way I think. When I walk into the room and change the channel, I am not intentionally imposing my will on others. Rather, I am oblivious of the other people. I do not realize they are there, and with that realization lacking, there is nothing to stop me from changing the channel.

Why don't I notice? I've thought about that, and I think the answers are first, I often concentrate deeply, and when that happens, I'm oblivious to lots of things. Second, even if I do notice people, I often don't get their connection to something like the TV. Perhaps it's a body-language thing; perhaps it's just too abstract. If I do notice others or just "get it," and that happens sometimes, I leave the TV alone.

Outside the TV room, I'm essentially a loner, so my plans pretty much involve me and me alone. Once I get outside the circle of my family and close friends, it does not occur to me to include other people in most situations. If other people are included in my plans, it's because they are cooperating with me, not because I am exploiting them in a predatory way.

I realize that I often get into trouble when I implement my solitary plans and someone else unwittingly gets in my way. To that person, I look like the nypical who's trying to take advantage, when in reality I didn't even know he or she was there. It doesn't help to try explaining myself, because not knowing someone was there can be just as much of an insult as deliberately taking advantage. That's been a hard problem for me, because it goes right to my Aspergian social weakness.

It seems that nypicals are more aware of their surroundings, especially in a social sense. I've already talked about how I miss subtle expressions in other people. This issue of self-centeredness makes me realize that sometimes I don't even notice the other person at all! It must be awful to be totally ignored by someone else when he is standing right next to you. And I don't even know I'm doing it.

Nypicals may take in a roomful of people by instinct, but I can achieve a pretty decent result by using good old focus and concentration.

I wanted friends, and I didn't want people to perceive me as something I'm not, so I resolved to develop a workaround for that deficiency.

I've made a lot of headway with that in recent years. Nypicals may take in a roomful of people by instinct, but I can achieve a pretty decent result by using good old focus and concentration, just as I do with reading people's emotions. When I walk into a room, I now make a point of looking at and noting every person. Sometimes I'll say something. Other times a quick glance is all it takes. That simple step of establishing a connection to others is crucial. It reduces the chance that I'll do something wrong out of ignorance, and it opens the door for people to greet me or otherwise draw me into their circle.

I suspect that the importance of initial connection is the reason nypicals evolved the hand-shaking ceremony. By shaking hands with everyone when you enter a room, you make a connection to them and avoid the "I never noticed you" problem. I never did that before, preferring to slink into a room quietly and stand in a corner. Now I embrace the handshake routine wholeheartedly, and it really works. I might get a few more diseases from all the skin contact, but hey, that's what hand washing is for.

Simply making myself aware of others has remarkably improved in my social life. People accept me much faster now that I ignore them less. The change is dramatic.

This process is a secret of my success, one that helped turn me from a self-centered loner into a pleasant eccentric with a number of friends. To me, that's pretty good progress. And the cost has not been great. I can still watch those television shows; I just ask first now. Sometimes the people say yes, and sometimes they squeal and I switch the channel anyway. But even when I do that, it's okay, because somehow it's not insulting anymore, now that I acknowledge the people around me. The only problem I've found with focusing on the other people in a room is that it's mentally exhausting. Nypical party animals may go till three in the morning on instinct; I'm worn out by ten. But I'll take fewer hours and more friends any day.

It's a constant source of amazement to me, how important something like simple social acknowledgment can be to others, while being totally invisible to me all these years.

The Art of Conversation

I'm blessed with excellent language skills. My vocabulary, grammar, and diction have always been far above average for my age. Yet all through grammar school, when it came to using those wonderful skills to win friends and influence people, I fell flat on my face. Luckily, that situation improved as I got older. One key to success proved to be acquiring some wisdom. Language came to me naturally, with no apparent effort. Wisdom, on the other hand, was really tough to obtain.

One key to success proved to be acquiring some wisdom.

The first big piece of wisdom came about at age ten, when I made a life-changing discovery. I figured out that I had to make "context-sensitive" replies in conversation. For example, if I was playing solitaire on the card table at school, and Ben Parker came up to tell me about his new bicycle, I had to say something about bicycles in response.

Before that revelation, if Ben said, "Look at my bike," I would have answered, "I have three aces." Looking back, I can see that those two statements don't go together, though my response made perfect sense to me in light of what I was doing. Why should I have to talk about *his* topic? I was playing cards, and Ben had approached me. Logic suggests that Ben should have walked up and said something like, "Neat game of solitaire you're playing!" He shouldn't have talked about his bike at all until the conversation got going.

Yet that never happened. Kids walked up to me and said, "Look at my bike," or whatever was on their minds. And they expected me to answer whatever weird thing they said. It sure seemed illogical and unfair. I didn't comply, and the interaction broke down. Usually, I ended up alone, without the hope of a new friend.

Today, if Ben said, "Look at my bike," I would reply, "Nice bike. I like that seat," and the conversation would take off. "Nice bike" is a correct contextual response; "Look at my helicopter" is not. Now that I understand, it's obvious. But it was not obvious before.

What a simple and powerful conversational rule that is: You should respond to what others say, not just speak what's on your mind. Teachers had been explaining that to me for years, but until I was about ten I didn't recognize that other kids had thoughts and feelings that

> *You should respond to what others say, not just speak what's on your mind.*

were fully independent of my own. When I finally figured all that out, I made a big leap forward socially.

I learned a few other things by the time I entered junior high. For example, big words were problematic for me. I knew I had a good vocabulary—all the grown-ups said so—but big words turned out to be another tricky aspect of dialogue. Though adults were impressed when I used words like "prognostication" or "reciprocity" or coined a witty turn of phrase, like "You can lead a horse to water, but a pencil must be lead," the response of kids was much less consistent. Some laughed at my cleverness, while others laughed at me. A few smart kids threw their own big words right back at me until it felt like a contest to see who had the most esoteric language.

I could usually win those contests, because I was blessed with the ability to make up big words, like "repugnatron," and then use them in some totally made-up context that no one else understood, but which sounded believable anyway. I had a lot of kids believing that repugnatrons converted sewage and lawn waste into edible foods in New York City cafeterias.

Even though I won the contests, I knew I was losing the war. I realized that my use of big words and complex phrases set me apart from the other kids. Instead of helping me to fit in, my sophisticated speech isolated me. To solve the problem, I fell back on my grandfather's sage advice: Listen to what the others do, and act like them. I became something of a chameleon of language, talking like a little professor when I was among the real professors at my parents' college, and talking like a little thug in the Amherst High School garage.

Some of my classmates didn't use any words longer than five letters and didn't understand any word longer than six. I initially followed the lead of grown-ups, interpreting certain kids' poor speaking skills as a sign of their diminished intelligence. But as I realized that many kids with marginal speech skills often had fascinating interests and abilities, I became hesitant about making that assumption.

The guys in the auto shop were a good example. "You can recognize greasers by the well-developed muscles in their heads" was how my friend Juke described them, meaning they had muscle instead of brains in their skulls. He may have acted contemptuous toward them, but those greasers could do things like tune a carburetor and set up an engine—things I just dreamed of at that age.

I might have known lots of big words, but the engines they worked on were far superior to the bicycles I tinkered with. That's why I decided to look beyond their poor grammar and limited vocabulary. There were things in that shop that I needed to understand.

Once I began talking their language, I got to know a few kids in the shop, and I learned for sure that they weren't stupid at all. They sounded rough, but they were actually quite intelligent.

"You guys sound pretty stupid, but you are actually smart" may have been an accurate expression of my feelings about the guys in the shop, but by the time I was able to communicate with them I had luckily come to my third important realization: There are times when it's better to keep your mouth shut.

"If you don't have anything nice to say," my grandmother said, "just keep your thoughts to yourself. You'll never get

> *There are times when it's better to keep your mouth shut.*

into trouble if you follow that rule." I made a mental note of the kinds of things I should not say to people, even when they were true. These are the things I do not say. I do not tell people they are

fat
foul smelling
revolting
stupid
really weird looking
or anything else of that ilk

In fact, I distilled all those things into one simple rule: Do not talk about someone else's appearance unless it's a compliment. Even if I am really, really curious about the disgusting pus-filled sore on Fred's cheek, I know it's best to not mention it. If I am lucky, Fred will volunteer the whole gross story, but if he stays quiet, so do I. It's better that way, but it's hard to be quiet when goo starts dripping off his cheek.

In addition, I do not compare other people unfavorably to myself, even though the comparison may be apt. I know from hard experience that saying, "I could do that better when I was seven" may well be true, but the statement virtually guarantees a bad outcome to the conversation.

There are instances, though, when it's not clear if someone will take what you say as an insult or as a compliment. For example, if I say, "You look really pregnant" to a girl who is merely overweight, she might turn vicious. But if she is pregnant, she will be complimented. The outcome hinges on my guessing ability, which isn't too good.

There are people with greater social sensitivity who can handle conversations like that, but I am not one of them. I find it best to just talk to the person without commenting on her appearance. That's almost always safe, especially when dealing with females.

And that brings me to my last learned rule of conversation: I have to be a lot more careful around females than around males. There are certain conversational missteps that seem to provoke hostile reactions only from girls. Anyone will be insulted if I say, "Jeez, you sure smell bad today." But females can also get insulted if I don't praise them, whereas guys don't generally expect compliments.

I have to be a lot more careful around females than around males.

For example, I remember my first girlfriend getting mad at me one day. We were talking about Larry Niven's new book, *Ringworld*. She seemed to be getting snippier, and I could not figure out what was wrong. Finally, she blurted it out. "I cut my hair, and you didn't even notice!"

It was true. I had not noticed. Was that a failure of conversation, or a failure to notice? I now believe it was both. I am not very observant about changes in other people. Haircuts and changes of clothing style usually pass right over my head. My friends have come to know and accept it. But I have learned that new acquaintances and especially girls may hold me to a higher standard in that regard, so I pay closer attention to what I say when I'm around them.

I taught myself to look for nice things I can say, things that are somewhat complimentary without seeming over the top or fake. That can be dicey, because many positive adjectives tend to be taken the wrong way. For example, "You smell clean today" seldom goes over well. I said that to a girl once, and instead of thanking me, she responded, "Why, did I smell bad last time?" I used to have a problem with questions like that, because I felt I had to tell the whole truth, which might be something like, "No, but you smelled really bad last Tuesday and Wednesday." Truthful answers like that led to trouble. Now I know I can say something like, "That's not what I meant. Smelling good today doesn't mean you smelled bad yesterday!" Even if she did smell bad, my statement is still true, and it saves the conversation.

Today, I understand that the whole testy exchange can be avoided with an innocuous "You look nice today." For some reason, I can say a girl looks nice and it's a compliment, whereas praising her for smelling clean is chancy and open to challenge.

A guy would never respond that way. Girls are the trickiest and most unpredictable creatures a fellow like me will ever talk to.

Lobster Claws:
Dealing with Bullies

Don Mclean sat in front of me in Mr. Styspeck's chemistry class in eighth grade. I wasn't friends with Don before that class, though I knew who he was. Don was a quiet kid, but he did some annoying things. One was throwing spitballs. He'd roll up these disgusting wads of wet paper in his grubby damp hands and toss them back over his head when he thought I wasn't looking. What kind of animal would do that?

The worst part was when a cold wet chunk of paper landed on my face. It was revolting. I imagined breathing in a spitball, the way I occasionally inhaled bugs. Gross. I used a clean piece of paper to wipe it off, after which I discreetly flicked it off my desk with a fingernail. Which I then wiped clean on my pants leg, many times over.

I sat there behind Don, silently stewing and wondering what to do about the situation. What grown-up could I turn to? My grandfather always stood up for me, but he was a thousand miles away in Georgia. My parents were no use; they were wrapped up in their own craziness. The teachers didn't like me or didn't care, and I didn't trust them anyway. Experience had shown me that all I could count on from the school was punishment after the fact. If I told a teacher about Don, she'd say, "Now, Don. Be nice," and he'd just laugh and act even worse because I had ratted him out to a teacher. As much as I wished otherwise, this was a problem for me to solve on my own.

I considered acids and poisons, like I'd read about in Sherlock Holmes stories, but I was afraid they'd just get me into bigger trouble. A few days passed. He continued spitballing, and I continued pondering. Something had to change. And it did, when he decided to escalate things.

He started pinching.

I was not his only target; I wasn't even the first. His proclivity for the pinch first appeared as we stood in a group watching an experiment.

"Hey!" The yelp came from Holly, who was standing a few feet away from me. "He pinched me," she said, pointing at Don. Don backed away, smiling slightly, and class continued. From that moment on, I watched him even closer than before. But not closely enough. One day I felt a sharp bite in my lower back, and I spun around to see him backpedaling slowly with

I didn't yell, but I resolved to do something. But what? Extermination was too extreme a punishment.

a smug expression. I didn't yell, but I resolved to do something.

But what? Extermination was too extreme a punishment. Suddenly, the answer came to me. Pliers. As soon as I got the idea, I couldn't wait to get home and examine my toolbox.

Later that day I stood over the box, reviewing my options. The wire cutters would do a job on him, but I'd surely get in trouble if I cut off a finger or an ear. Ear removal was too extreme a response to a pinch. Even I could see that. With some reluctance, I put them aside. I picked up the regular pliers. *Too blunt,* I thought. I couldn't grab him under his shirt or pants. That's when I saw what I needed: needle-nose pliers. They were just the thing. Able to reach through clothing, but not sharp enough to sever big pieces of kid. I brought them to school the next day.

When I sat down in chemistry class I felt a renewed confidence. No more would I be the victim of bullying. I waited, and my chance was not long in coming. A spitball landed on my desk, right in the middle of my class paper. Don sat there smugly, not even turning around. I slid the pliers out of my pocket and reached forward. I grabbed a good chunk of kid through his shirt, and I gave a hard pull and a twist. The response was immediate.

"Oooooooooooooooooooooooooooooooooooow!" He gave a very satisfying howl and erupted right out of his seat and onto the floor. He turned to see what had grabbed him, and I gave a friendly smile of acknowledgment. I snapped the pliers like a lobster claw, indicating there was plenty more where the first bite came from. He backed away like I was some kind of poisonous snake. Mission accomplished.

Unfortunately, his howling and carrying on attracted the attention of the teacher. I found myself packed off to the office to face the Lord of Discipline, also known as the assistant principal.

"Well," he said, "what do you have to say for yourself?" I had recently learned about the U.S. Constitution, which I had originally thought was just an old wooden ship tied to a dock in Boston's Charlestown Navy Yard. I knew it contained this provision called the Fifth Amendment, which meant I did not have to answer him. So I didn't.

My expression was backward for the situation, but I was powerless to change it.

However, I could not help showing the slightest of grins on my face. That drove the Lord of Discipline wild. The madder he got, the more I grinned. Within a moment, he was almost shouting and I was almost laughing. It seemed like his anger produced the opposite effect in me, and I just kept grinning more.

Yet I knew my expression could get me into even more trouble. I wasn't really amused; being yelled at by a belligerent assistant principal wasn't fun or funny at all. My expression was backward for the situation, but I was powerless to change it.

I've thought long and hard about why that was, because it's happened to me many times since that day. I think I smiled because my brain interpreted what was going on in the context of me and me alone. As I stood before the Lord of Discipline, I figured I had good reason to rejoice. I had beaten an obnoxious pest and a bully, and I had every right to be relieved and pleased.

The trouble was, the assistant principal expected some expression of remorse from me, and it just wasn't there. He thought he could yell at me for what I'd done, and I would feel bad, just like that! *Why? Why should I feel bad for Don, just because he was whining down the hall, in the nurse's office? I didn't torment other kids like he did! Far from remorse, I felt PRIDE! I'd faced down a bully, and won!*

None of the grown-ups ever saw into my mind to understand how I felt and why I acted as I did. They just took my behavior as evidence of my psychopathy, sociopathy, or general evilness. That was really bad, both for them and for me. They were convinced that I was a little monster, waiting to go out and savage the world. Meanwhile, I was just a kid trying to protect myself. What did I know?

(Those adults and their incorrect interpretations of my behavior had a corrosive effect on my self-image that lasted for years. Well into adulthood, I was haunted by the possibility that I might be a serial killer waiting to emerge. No amount of gentle behavior on my part cured me of that ugly nagging fear, even though I never hurt anyone or anything.)

I've had many experiences like that, when people expect me to show remorse or distress or sadness, and I just can't. Maybe I'm too logical, or maybe that part of my brain is simply weak. But when I see someone I care for come to harm, my feelings for them are very strong. I don't have any weakness at all in that regard; it's just a question of what triggers my response.

In any case, the Lord of Discipline finally gave up on me that long-ago day. He had to do something, so my mother was called, and I was sent home for the day, victorious. That was the last time Don bothered me, or anyone else in that class. He became, as they say, meek as a lamb.

A diplomat would call my actions a proportionate response. There were lots of things I could have done in response to Don's tormenting. My choice was reasonable in light of the situation and Don's actions, and it worked. A weaker response may have failed, and put me in a worse situation. A stronger response might have gotten me in trouble with the law. It's all a matter of balance.

Modern-day teachers assure me that I'd get expelled for using pliers on Don today, but things were different in 1970. One thing, though, has not changed. Bullies are still bullies, and whatever you may think of my tactics, they worked. Unfortunately, they won't work for everyone. You can read about my problems in these pages, but one thing you can't get from reading was my size. I was always a big kid, and walking six miles to school most days made me pretty strong. By the time I got to high school, I was one of the biggest kids in my class; I was far from being the class weakling, even though my self-image made me feel that way at times. As a result, I was able to stand up for myself in a direct and physical way that might have left a smaller kid battered and bruised.

I wish I had more answers to the problems of bullying, especially in today's world, where much of the bullying is online—ethereal and hard to trace and fight. In the end, my best advice is this:

> *Learn to coexist peacefully. Even if you can't make friends, don't make enemies.*
>
> *Don't tease, torment, or provoke other people. Don't be a bully yourself.*
>
> *Try to understand the other person, and by doing so, make a peaceful connection.*
>
> *If people tease or torment you, look first to strong adults for help.*
>
> *Finally, if all else fails you may have to take a stand. And when you do, know that you could be putting yourself in harm's way. But whatever happens, you will have stood up for yourself and what you believe, and that is a path to success, hard as it sounds.*

I wish there were a better answer to this age-old problem, but there isn't.

(A few years later, inspired by my actions, the Firesign Theatre released a record called *Don't Crush That Dwarf, Hand Me the Pliers*. You should check it out.)

Animal Wariness

The older I got, the more my long history of failed interactions with other people weighed on me. I became chronically sad and angry, skating on the edge of depression. I began to expect and even anticipate failure or rejection.

I became wary, especially of large groups of people. *Some of them are probably unfriendly,* I'd remind myself. *I'd better watch out.*

Looking back, I realize that I could stay calm when I was surrounded by my family or in groups of twenty to thirty kids, the usual pack size I encountered in nursery school and elementary school. A few became my friends, more became acquaintances, and a few had to be watched. All in all, it was manageable. I did not fear recess or going to school. The other kids may not have been my buddies, but they weren't my enemies, either. I didn't know how to make friends, but I did learn to avoid fights by staying mostly to myself, not grabbing other kids' stuff, and not calling them names.

Not making enemies is a distinct skill in its own right, and I began to master it when I learned to keep calm and quiet and to mind my own business.

That was a vital skill I had learned by elementary school—how to not make enemies. Some people think it's automatic, or somehow goes with making friends, but they're wrong. Not making enemies is a distinct skill in its own right, and I began to master it when I learned to keep calm and quiet and to mind my own business.

Things changed when I went into seventh grade. I went from a small-town primary school to a regional junior high, with seven hundred kids. It was huge, and I didn't know anyone. Most of the kids were from Amherst, the largest town in the district, and many had been together since nursery school in the Amherst system. Being from Shutesbury, I was an outsider, in more ways than one.

Every day, when I got on the bus, I felt like Lloyd Bridges, the scuba diver in *Sea Hunt,* swimming out of his submerged steel cage into shark-infested seas. When I looked out at the mass of kids in the lunchroom, I saw an amorphous mass of humanity. Hundreds of them, roiling and teeming, like a school of fish. But there was a big difference between the star of *Sea Hunt* and me. He was big, and he had a speargun. I was thirteen years old, and totally unarmed. I was also essentially alone. My elementary school was so small, it sent only a dozen seventh graders to Amherst Regional. We were all lost. With seven hundred other kids around us, we were truly in the belly of the beast.

Most of the new kids were harmless. One or two even liked me. But I quickly discovered I was right to be wary. Sprinkled throughout the crowd were a number of bad seeds . . . sneak thieves, bullies, and predators. At any moment, they could pounce on me. The danger was there, but I was always ready. I'd learned how you should handle yourself: Never let down your guard. Always watch your surroundings. Look left, right, and behind. And if you're outdoors, look up, too. Predators can jump from trees.

Walking through Amherst Regional School, I employed the same senses and skills that I used to stay safe from poisonous snakes and alligators in the swamps behind my grandparents' home in Georgia. None of those threats ever reached me, despite being nearby every summer day. I had a deadly water moccasin drop right into my rowboat one hot August day, but he didn't get me. *And these kids won't get me either,* I resolved. I kept all my senses wide open. Eyes, ears, and nose. And that sixth sense I had for danger, the one that knew what happened when

My ability to read faces may have been poor, but my ability to sense movement and danger was extraordinarily good.

the woods went all silent. My ability to read faces may have been poor, but my ability to sense movement and danger was extraordinarily good.

Some of the kids had reputations—I learned that as I watched and listened. I remember one in particular. He had a name, but no one used it. Everyone called him Blob. He was a belligerent slug, and if you saw him coming toward you, it was sure to mean trouble.

"Whatcha got there?" Blob would sound friendly as he sat down next to some hapless kid and picked up his dessert. "Tasty," he'd say as he started to eat it. His victim would freeze, afraid to fight back.

Blob tended to pick on scrawnier kids. I was skinny, but I sure wasn't weak. Thanks to my animal wariness, I was ready the day he sat down at my table.

He always seemed to pounce when the cafeteria served chocolate cake with white frosting. It must have been his favorite. Trouble was, it was my favorite, too, and I wasn't giving up my cake without a fight. He sat down next to me, looked me in the eye, and slid his arm across the table.

Smack! I brought the sharp edge of my notebook down on his wrist as hard as I could. As Blob cried out and shook his wrist, I kicked back from the table, jumped up, and got ready to nail him if he moved from his seat. To my surprise, he backed down instantly. "Hey, man! It's cool! Calm down!" He slid away slowly as the buzz of conversation around us began again.

The tables had suddenly turned. I sat down and resumed my watch for predators.

It took a lot of energy to be on guard every moment at school, but that's what I had to do. I think the other kids sensed it after a while. I gave off a vibe. It said: *This one is not good to eat.*

Something remarkable actually happened with Blob after that day. He became friendly to me, and almost went out of his way to talk to me. At first I thought his friendliness was false, but then I wasn't so sure. I engaged when he spoke to me, though I always kept my distance. I never saw him snicker at me like he did at some of the other kids. Some kids just don't respect you till you stand up for yourself. Blob and I didn't become real friends, but he never gave me a bit of trouble after that day.

By holding my tongue and holding my ground, I got through school without any fights or indeed any serious incidents at all, with the exception of my own pranks. And none of them were violent.

The wariness I acquired as a kid followed me into adulthood. It was a strain, but when I think of some of the places I went and some of the people I hung out with, it was probably a blessing that I had it. People saw that I never backed down, so they didn't push me.

In that manner, I got older and started a business. As I moved into creative and technical work, I also moved away from bullies. It seemed like the bullies from my youth made some fundamentally different career decisions, because I seldom saw those kinds of people in the places I went now. Life became more comfortable. I seldom felt threatened.

In high school I was like a soldier in wartime, on patrol

There are schools around now that control bullying and other threats, where students, even the wary ones, feel like they're in a safe haven.

and waiting to be ambushed. It's an exhausting way to live. But it doesn't have to be that way. There are schools around now that control bullying and other threats, where students, even the wary ones, feel like they're in a safe haven.

The first school where I really felt a sense of safety was Monarch School, in Houston, Texas. They specialize in programs for kids with neurological differences. I spoke there a few years ago, and was immediately struck by the peaceful environment. It was evident as soon as I stepped through the doors. The whole place felt gentle. And in that safe world, the kids did not have the cornered-animal look. The difference between them and me in high school was striking. Being there made me wish there had been schools like that when I was a kid. Maybe I wouldn't have felt the need to leave in tenth grade.

For that realization, the Monarch School awarded me an honorary high school diploma in May of 2008. So I'm not a tenth-grade dropout anymore. I'm a high school graduate, thirty-some years too late. All I need now is an honorary doctorate from some prestigious college, like Harvard or Yale or the University of Idaho, and I'll be one hundred percent legit.

Getting Chosen
(and Becoming Choosable)

How was I supposed to get a girlfriend, when I was a total nerd with no social skills? That was the pressing question for me and all my geek friends. We talked about it all the time, but the girlfriend problem seemed incredibly intractable and totally resistant to the application of logic or reason.

By age sixteen I had overcome many of my earlier limitations. I knew how to share. I could even sit quietly while the kid next to me did something totally wrong and made a complete mess. I'd learned where to find other geeks like me, places like the computer labs or the University Science Fiction Society. In those rooms it was easy to strike up a conversation with other guys, because we had stuff in common. Trouble was, there weren't very many females in those places, and the ones that were there always seemed taken by some lucky geek.

We were able to watch those fortunate fellows for ideas, but that was dicey. If you watched too closely, you were a stalker or a perv. Still, through careful and discreet observation my friends and I formed some theories on Girlfriend Acquisition. I also got ideas from my nongeek friends, many of whom had mastered GA by that time.

> *I didn't know about Asperger's back then, but you didn't need to understand psychiatry to separate the geeks from the nypicals when it came to dealing with girls.*

I didn't know about Asperger's back then, but you didn't need to understand psychiatry to separate the geeks from the nypicals when it came to dealing with girls. Nypicals were successful, whereas geeks were not. My friend Denny was a nypical, but we were buddies because he lived right next door and we rode the bus together every day. Otherwise, he probably would have turned up his nose at a kid like me.

"Just walk up to a girl and start talking to her. Ask her about her English assignment or invite her to sit with you at lunch." That sounded pretty easy. I even watched him do it. "Go ahead," he said. "Try it!" I resolved to do what he said, but when I started toward a girl, I found myself seized with terror. I was unable to move, unable to talk. Needless to say, the female escaped and I was left with a new respect, envy, even, for Denny's confidence and courage.

By this time I had developed a rule of thumb for how other boys would respond to me. If they were clean, neat, and popular, they would not want anything to do with me.

If they were geeks—freaky looking, with wild hair, mismatched socks, and inch-thick glasses—they would probably be friendly to me. If they were greasy or smelly, I avoided them. I didn't want to be around grubby kids, because I was wary of crabs, head lice, and poisonous body odors.

There were a decent number of geeks at Amherst High. It was truly unfortunate that they were all guys. All the guy friends in the world didn't add up to one girlfriend. I knew it, they knew it, and we were all frustrated. The worst thing was, we suspected there were similar numbers of lonely females, but we had no idea how to identify or reach them. It was a terrible and desperate situation.

> *All the guy friends in the world didn't add up to one girlfriend.*

The popular guys always had girls on their arms. I'd see couples walking together in the halls, and I'd feel sad and wistful. Sometimes I saw them holding hands, and I wondered what that would be like. I had not held anyone's hand since I was a little boy. How I wished I could do that.

When I was lucky enough to gain a female friend in those days (by some miracle), we were too shy to be boyfriend and girlfriend. In eighth grade I had made friends with Mary Trompke, whom I called Little Bear. We were together all the time, it seemed. I walked her home from school every day, then turned around and walked seven miles back to my own house. All that time, though, we never held hands or kissed. I thought about it, and I'm sure she did, too, but it was just too scary. We didn't go beyond that until we were both out of high school and she was at the University of Massachusetts. She later became my first wife, and our son Cubby's mom.

I didn't know it at the time, but Little Bear was a little bit autistic, too. Were we drawn to each other because of that? Surely our mutual social oblivion kept our budding romance moving at a glacial pace. Could we see kindred spirits in our difference? Whatever the reason, my connection to her has endured for almost forty years, which is more than I can say for most of the other people in my life.

Today, I can see why I didn't have other regular girlfriends in school. The simple answer is: I ran them off. I acted strange, and my antics dissuaded interested people from taking the next step. For example, I think Emily Bolduc wanted to make friends when she walked up to me after social studies class back in ninth grade. But when I looked at her and went, "Bow bow bow," like some kind of crazed dog, she quickly changed her mind. Who knows what might have been had I just responded in a less unexpected fashion.

The first girlfriend of my adult life— Cathy Moore— chose me while I was working with bands.

The first girlfriend of my adult life—Cathy Moore—chose me while I was working with bands, doing sound in local bars and clubs. That relationship didn't last, but it gave me confidence that I could make friends with girls and that I might not be alone forever. However, the road from there to marital contentment remained pretty rocky. Cathy showed me the value of basic manners, something I'll be forever grateful for. I also learned not to say totally weird things, which made me acceptable to a much wider circle of people. But I remained a social ignoramus, light-years removed from the popular kids I saw around me.

I bumbled along in that state right through into my early twenties. That was when I decided to get a real job. I became a staff engineer at Milton Bradley, the famous toy and game company in East Longmeadow, Massachusetts. That was the first time since high school that I found myself among lots of people, interacting with them about different things on a daily basis. Most people have that experience in college, but I didn't go to college, so I missed that opportunity for socialization.

Milton Bradley actually had behavioral standards and a dress code, which meant that I needed a major overhaul before walking in the door. I had read about Big Business and how one dressed for it, so I cleaned myself up for the first job interview and stayed on my best behavior right through the process.

The result of cutting six inches of extra hair and putting on a suit was just amazing. People reacted to me as if I were a different person. Before, I had looked like the factory workers, the mechanics, and all the others who did the physical work. Now, I found myself a part of the white-collar workforce. Executives actually addressed me in a different tone of voice than the one used to talk to the factory labor-ers. In some cases older people even deferred to me, not knowing I was little more than a big kid in a suit.

I was shocked to discover how powerful an impression clothes made. But once I saw it, I embraced the concept. As soon as I could afford it, I outfitted myself with a Brooks Brothers suit, Hathaway shirts, Bally shoes, and even ac-cessories like an S. T. Dupont fountain pen. I became a picture of sartorial elegance.

My new attire—and the manners I'd been picking up—also helped my social life. By looking like a young executive, I became acceptable to other young executives, and I was drawn into their society with very little effort on my part. By then, I had learned enough to watch and imitate, and I didn't run my new acquaintances off by howling, "Bow bow *bow!*" I couldn't play golf or do all the things they did, but I'd learned to nod politely, follow along, and stay in the group anyway.

After all, I'd overcome my fear of monsters. . . . Could it be that girls were scarier than T. rex? I guess they were.

However, even in the new and improved environ-ment, I was still not able to approach females. I'd been too scared to ask a girl to dance in junior high; now I was unable to ask an attrac-tive girl at work to lunch. Why were girls so scary? After all, I'd overcome my fear of monsters. . . . Could it be that girls were scarier than T. rex? I guess they were.

I was not the only geeky young adult with those fears. Bob Jeffway was another Milton Bradley engineer who felt exactly the same way. He and I both looked at the attractive females at work, but that was as far as it went. All we could do was admire them from a distance, or program a toy robot to approach them and report back. We watched movies and read books about it, but neither of us had the courage or confidence or polish to actually get a girl out on a date.

However, both of us were saved from loneliness by virtue of being chosen. Having females choose us rendered our own inability to pursue and choose potential mates moot. Becoming Choosable proved to be the solution to the Girlfriend Problem.

Bob was introduced to Celeste—the female who picked and married him—through a family friend. Celeste also happened to work at Milton Bradley, though they didn't actually meet there. I was reconnected with Little Bear, by chance, when we found each other as young adults at the University of Massachusetts. Both Bob and I ended up marrying our choosers, though it worked out better for Bob than for me, because he's still married to his and I'm not.

I recently asked Celeste what she had found attractive in Bob, and she said, "He was just the most interesting man I knew. Other guys just wanted to talk sports, but Bob was into airplanes and computers and all manner of things. He was just interesting." I was fascinated by that because all through high school it was the sports guys who got all the attention. Where were girls like Celeste in high school? After speaking with a few other females who chose geeks as mates, I concluded that preferences like hers must evolve after high school. They say a taste for fine wine is acquired in adulthood; perhaps more sophisticated mate-picking abilities arrive then, too.

> *When I made myself receptive to approaches from strangers I began making new friends, one after the other.*

What else did we do to get picked? you may ask. Well, I, for one, learned manners. Both of us learned more about how to behave so as not to shock or horrify others. We dressed well and placed ourselves among potential mates.

Once I learned I had Asperger's, I was able to make an even bigger leap in social acceptability because I understood how some of my behaviors affected other people. I realized I still had a number of obnoxious habits, like talking over people, running on and on, and general rudeness. Unfortunately, they were pretty ingrained, so they were hard to change. But I succeeded, and people responded almost immediately. When I made myself receptive to approaches from strangers I began making new friends, one after the other. I was amazed to discover that I really was a nice guy, or at least a reasonably likable one.

I learned that it was possible to make friends with a girl without asking her to dance, or doing things that seemed unnatural to either of us. Best of all, I figured out how to get girls and guys to approach me, just by being myself. I guess you could say I learned to be the human equivalent of a flower. Just by being there, flowers attract honeybees.

Today I know that the things I do in the course of my life are interesting to other people. So rather than focus on how to make people like me, I focus on how to do the things I do really well. I still don't know how to ask a girl to dance, but I do know how to be a good restorer of cars and a good designer of sound systems. So I go out and do those things, and more, every day. That's who I am. And now I know that people will like me for those real accomplishments, if only I open myself to their approach. I call that *being receptive*.

I still can't really go out and actually chase down new friends, but making myself receptive to other people's approaches has brought me many new friendships. For someone like me, that seems to be a good strategy. As successful as I am, I still have not let go of some fundamental insecurities. By being the chosen, not the chooser, I reduce the risk that someone will laugh in my face and call me names. People come to me because I did something that captured their interest, and not vice versa, so most of the anxiety is on them.

Be Different

What a wonderful idea!

Some people have told me, "Your idea of getting chosen is nutty. I can go meet anyone I want." That may be true for some people, but it's not true for me. I can do interesting things. I can display good manners and look clean and presentable. The most important thing I can do is to make myself receptive. All those things will incline people to approach me. However, none of that empowers me to walk up to a stranger and attempt to make friends. I just can't do it, not without some kind of context.

That means my circle of friends is limited to those who first display an interest in me. I'm a chosen, not a chooser. That sounds restrictive, but it's really not. For a relationship to succeed, both people must choose each other. And it has to start with someone. I must choose you, or you must choose me. It doesn't matter who makes the initial approach. There are millions of people in the world, and if I present myself properly, plenty of them will chose to connect with me.

You can do it, too. Take regular showers, wear clean clothes, brush your hair, and mind those manners. Listen more and talk less. All that may seem like a waste of time, but I assure you, the results are worth it.

Let the friendships begin.

Part 4

Tuned In: Sensitivity to the Nonhuman World

It's true that nypicals have strong instincts when it comes to reading other people's emotions. But Aspergians often have the ability to see and read nonhuman aspects of the world around us in a unique way.

I've always possessed special gifts that nypicals don't seem to have access to. I'm able to see and feel all the components of music and machines, instinctually. I also perceive shifts in the natural world through a deep connection with the landscape. Wind changes, animals' movements, they all say something to me. At times, my ability to "tune in" is harmful, like when I can feel a seam on my clothes rubbing against my skin all day or when a small background noise takes over my brain.

These chapters shine some light on my unique insights, both when they are helpful and when they hold me back. I hope you connect my stories to what's happening in your own life and the lives of those around you.

Underwear with Teeth

Can you feel the labels on your underwear right now? I can. I can also feel the seams on the inside of my shirt and pants. At this very moment, the tags in the collar of my shirt are gnawing at my neck. Luckily, I have taught myself to ignore those feelings most of the time. Otherwise, they would drive me crazy.

I know a rational designer would not incorporate the functional equivalent of sandpaper into his own underwear or create clothes with seams that scratched and clawed him every time he got dressed, so I've come to the conclusion that I am unusually sensitive to certain kinds of touch.

> *I've come to the conclusion that I am unusually sensitive to certain kinds of touch.*

Unfortunately, knowing I am different does not make me more comfortable. I still have to endure constant assault from seams and labels on clothing. Even the fabric itself can become aggressive.

Psychiatrists tell me that many people on the autism spectrum have unusual sensitivities. Some—like me—are sensitive to touch. Others are sensitive to sound, or light, or even smell. A few of us are sensitive to everything.

Touch sensitivity has its good points, but it can also bother me a lot, especially when I think about it. As I write this passage, my clothing is becoming increasingly noticeable. Sharp little fibers are biting into my back. The label on my shirt is scratching my neck. The more I think about it, the more I feel. Soon, I may have to tear all these clothes right off. Hopefully something will divert my attention before that happens. Otherwise, this shirt is headed for a bad end. But probably not. If this time is like most, some distraction will come along and my touch sensitivity will fade into the background.

Things were worse when I was younger. There were days when a piece of clothing would bother me all day, and I'd just sit there distracted and fidgeting. "Why are you squirming around like that?" my teachers would challenge me when they saw me wriggling. "Can't you sit still?" I never knew how to answer them, so I'd say something like, "I don't know," and they'd just get mad at me. For some reason, I never thought to say what was really bothering me. I knew I was itching, but for some reason, I could never seem to say that. I should have said, "My sweater is scratching me and I'm distracted." If I had, I'm sure my teacher would have understood. Maybe she'd have told me to take it off, or worked something else out. I wish I had known, but I just didn't get it.

"How could that be?" people ask me, dumbfounded. "How could you just sit there while a piece of clothing quietly drove you nuts?" As a child, I never knew why I suffered in silence. Years later, my crazy old pet poodle has provided the answer. Like many small dogs, he wears a harness rather than a simple collar. The harness has a loop around his neck, a loop around his chest, and a strap that holds the loops together. Every now and then, he gets tangled up in his harness. If you try to take it off him to free his leg, he'll bite. He must think that harness is a part of him, and when I try to take it away, he goes nuts, as if I were trying to cut off his tail.

I was the same way as a little kid. When my mom put an itchy wool sweater on me, it became a part of me, and it would never occur to me to just take it off because it itched. So it just drove me crazy, quietly.

Today I meet moms who cut the labels out of their kids' clothes and trim the seams. The first time I heard that, it sounded great. *What a nice thing to do*, I thought. But when I thought about things a little more, I began to question the wisdom of that. Why? Because removing the irritants doesn't do anything to decrease our sensitivity. And if clothes tags bother us today, and we don't address the nuisance head-on, where will we be in ten years? Naked at work?

Instead of fixing my clothes, I fixed myself. I learned to focus my mind so that my sense of touch no longer controlled me.

That statement sounds as if I decided one day to ignore

Be Different

I learned to focus my mind so that my sense of touch no longer controlled me.

those irritating labels and move on. That's not exactly what happened. It began with casual dismissal from my parents. When I complained about an itch, my father said, "Just ignore it. Think of something else." And my mother said, "John Elder, sometimes wool is itchy." I'm pretty sure my parents never shared my sensitivity to clothes, and so it never occurred to them to do anything to relieve my own distress. Eventually, I taught myself to think of other things, like my father told me. So how did I do it? As they say, it's all in the mind. . . .

I've learned that my senses are arranged by a kind of priority system in my head. When I'm awake, first place goes to vision, with sound a close second. Sights and sounds always seem to take precedence over touch and smell, unless the stench is really, really bad. The smell of a dead squirrel will trump an irritating lawn mower every time. But when there's nothing going on, those other senses perk up, and I begin noticing all sorts of little things that usually escape me. Touch rises to the top, and sometimes the annoyances begin.

I notice touch sensitivity most as I'm lying in bed at night, where it's dark and quiet. That's why I can't wear clothes to bed—the seams would keep me awake. Socks are the same way—I don't feel them during the day, when

I wear shoes, but late at night, my feet feel like they are wrapped in straitjackets if I go to bed wearing socks.

The older I've gotten, the easier it has become for me to ignore things like underwear labels. I've worked hard on training my mind in that way. But it's also easy to slip back, so I have to be careful. If I let myself feel a label's scratchy surface, it will take only a moment and some other sharp fragment of clothing will be digging at me somewhere else. Right now, it's a strand of jagged wool in the left sleeve of my sweater. It seems like every itch I feel in my clothes leads to another. If I let myself go down that road I'd have to live in a nudist colony, and I don't want to do that.

Brain scientists say things like this get stuck in our minds by a process called brain plasticity. Think of the sled runs you see on a hillside in winter. The more times you go down the hill, the more fixed the paths become. After a few days you've worn highways into the snow and those are the only places the sled will go. No matter where you start at the top of the hill, you fall into one of the well-worn grooves on the way to the bottom. So you always end up in the same place.

Your brain is the same way. Allow it to fixate on something like an annoying label, and pretty soon you'll be stuck because you can't get out of that track. Your brain will have formed a path, and every time your mind goes down it, the path gets wider and more worn in. The more times you go there, the harder it will be to erase. That's

Allow it to fixate on something like an annoying label, and pretty soon you'll be stuck because you can't get out of that track.

true for lots of things—not just clothing sensitivity.

Many kids, and indeed people of all ages, are sensitive to touch; it's not just an autistic thing. However, those of us on the spectrum are particularly susceptible to sensitivities like this because of how our brains are wired. Recent studies have shown that autistic people start out with more plasticity than nypicals, meaning our brains change more easily, and more profoundly, in response to life's experiences. There are times when this gives us an advantage in life, but touch sensitivity is an area where our plasticity can really work against us. That's why it's especially important that we flatten out those undesirable paths early in life. They can be really hard to get rid of when we get older.

I've had pretty good luck with that erasing. I was able to teach myself to ignore small scratchy things. It was a gradual process, teaching my mind to ignore the label and focus on something else, like the sound of the wind in the trees or even a show on television. One thing that helps is focusing my mind inward. First, I listen to the sound of wind if I'm outdoors. I try to relax, and breathe slowly. Then I start a metronome in my head. I imagine a chime sound, like a bell, repeating about once a second. I can

imagine it so clearly, it's almost as if it's really there, ringing next to me. I focus on that ding and the world recedes
a little bit. The more I focus, the less things like scratchy
clothes bother me. After a few minutes of concentration,
they seem to fade away and I feel more relaxed.

I've minimized my label sensitivity so well that I can
even wear rough wool sweaters. I could never do that when
I was fifteen. Now, having said all that, I'll tell you a secret.
I wear my underwear inside
out, so the irritating seams
and the label are on the
outside. And I never wear
designer underwear, be-
cause fancy brands have irritating labels on both sides,
and that's too much for me.

> *I've minimized my
> label sensitivity
> so well that I can
> even wear rough
> wool sweaters.*

Just because I can make myself ignore irritating clothing
doesn't mean I have to actually seek it out.

After all, I am not a masochist.

Seeing Music

I can still remember the first time I saw the music. It happened at a dance in the cafeteria at Amherst Regional Junior High. Ernie Buck and the Machines—a local high school band—were playing "Get Ready," a hit tune that had been recorded by both Rare Earth and the Temptations. The room was dark, loud, and full of kids. Light washed out from the stage, pushing aside the smell of sweat and socks. Colored shafts of light spun across the dance floor. You'd never guess we ate lunch there during the day.

"I'm bringing you a love that's true," Ernie sang. "So get ready!"

My neighbor Denny had insisted we go to the dance. He was a few months older than I, and a lot more popular and sophisticated. He even had a girlfriend, a brown-haired ninth grader named Brenda Keyes. I hoped I could learn from him and get a girlfriend of my own. I watched the other kids closely to see how it happened.

"Gonna start making love to you," the song continued.

Unfortunately, I wasn't having much luck in that department. Denny had explained the process to me, but I couldn't quite pull it off. "You just walk up to a girl and ask her to dance. Then she says yes, and follows you out to the dance floor. Afterward you can talk to her and make friends." I couldn't imagine how I could ever do such a thing, even as I watched other kids doing what he said.

I looked at the girls scattered around the room. Some were with guys—I ruled them out because they already had boyfriends hanging around. Even I knew that you didn't walk up to a girl who was with a guy and ask her to dance. That would be like asking for a fight. What about the girls who weren't with guys? Quite a few were standing together in packs, talking and laughing with one another. I figured they were out, too, because a pack of girls would tear me to shreds if I walked over and they didn't like my look. I could already see them laughing, and I didn't want to be the one getting laughed at. So I stayed away. That left the girls who were standing alone around the room. I didn't approach them, because I couldn't think of a single word to say, even though I'd been pondering what to say all day.

Finally, there was the problem of dancing. I could observe it, and understand intellectually how it worked, but to actually do it . . . never. I watched the kids on the dance floor, but there was no way I could ever move around like them.

So that was it. I figured there were no girls I could talk to or dance with. That just wasn't something I was going to be able to do. Freed from that worry, I retreated behind the stage, where I could watch the scene from a safe hiding place.

That's when I saw the music. It was there, in the backs of the amplifiers. Each musician had his own amp, and from my vantage point, I could see into the backs of their cabinets. Modern amplifiers are transistorized, and there's nothing to see. Back then, amplifiers used vacuum tubes, which glowed dimly and made patterns of light in time to the music.

> *That's when I saw the music. It was there, in the backs of the amplifiers.*

They were like windows to a secret realm, revealing the inner world of the dance hall. I leaned forward eagerly and gazed inside.

Girls were terrifying. The world of electronics was safe, predictable, and secure. Amplifiers never laughed at me. I had been fascinated—obsessed even—with electronics since my parents gave me a computer kit for Christmas the year before. I spent countless hours studying my computer and unraveling its secrets. As soon as I unraveled them I applied all my newfound knowledge to my other great love—music. By the time of the dance, I had already sacrificed every radio and television in the house to my pursuit of electrical knowledge. I was about to learn a new lesson.

Each amplifier had a mix of small and large tubes. The little tubes were important, but I knew it was the big ones that did the heavy lifting. They took the weak signals from the preamp tubes and made them strong enough to ring through the speaker cabinets and fill the room. When they did that, they pulsed with a faint blue glow whose shape and brightness changed with the music. I'd never seen that before and I was captivated. I put my face right up behind the bass amplifier—a Fender Bassman—sitting on top of a big black speaker cabinet. At that distance, the pounding of the bass was all I could hear. As I watched, the blue lights in the tubes danced in perfect synchronization with the sounds from the speaker below. At the same time, I felt waves of heat on my face whenever the bass played loudly. Sound poured from the speakers, and heat radiated from the tubes. It was a total sensory experience.

> *The longer I watched, the more the patterns revealed themselves.*

The longer I watched, the more the patterns revealed themselves. Chords had one shape, while individual notes had another. It felt magical, seeing the light dancing in the tubes as the energy of the music passed through. It appeared as light inside the amp, becoming invisible in the wires. The speakers turned the electrical energy to sound, and it rocked me back on my feet.

As the night wore on, the band played louder and louder. At times, they played so loudly that the amps overloaded. When that happened I could hear the distortion in the speakers and see bright bars in the blue lights. It was captivating, seeing the change. Undistorted sounds appeared as smooth patterns. Hard distortion made distinct bright bars. I forgot all about the dance, the girls, and the other people.

As the volume rose, something else happened. The dark metal on the outside of the tube began glowing dull red. The center was supposed to be red, because there was a heater there to make the tube work, but the rest of the tube was usually black. If the outside got red, that could mean only one thing. I was actually seeing metal get red hot as it passed the electricity on its way to the speakers. The thought of those tubes turning the tiny signals from an electric bass into a thunder that filled the room was thrilling. Would they melt? I felt the heat. Now I could smell the hot electronics, too.

My world shrank down to the tiny area inside those tubes. I watched them all night, until it was time to go home. I didn't get anywhere with the girls, but I had some revelations when it came to electronics.

The next day, I told one of the kids on the bus about my experience seeing music in the vacuum tubes. He looked at me like I was nuts. He said, "I almost got to third base with Cheryl Reed last night. With all the girls in that place you looked in the back of amplifiers? What's the matter with you?" We may have been in the same place physically, but our minds were light-years apart. How did that happen? I started out wanting to meet a girl, and I ended up watching vacuum tubes. Did the tubes distract me from loneliness, or was I so much of a geek that I actually forgot? I really didn't know.

I wasn't even sure what third base meant, though I deduced it involved a sex act. Unfortunately, if romance was a game with bases, I wasn't even at first. In any case, I did not want to focus on my failures with girls. Music was pure, safe, and immeasurably more promising because it had a logical mathematical foundation. That meant I could figure it out. Girls were not that way at all. I turned away and pondered the sounds and patterns in silence for the rest of the bus ride.

> *The technical terms didn't make much sense at first, but I kept reading until I understood. I was on my way.*

In the next few weeks I read everything I could find on vacuum tubes, in the *Encyclopaedia Britannica,* the *Radio Amateur's Handbook,* and the *RCA Receiving Tube Manual.* I wanted to know what made the blue glow, and why the tubes got red hot at the end of the night. I learned about anodes, cathodes, heaters, and plate current. Tiny signals on the grids controlled huge signals on the plates. That was the secret to amplification. It wasn't magic at all—it was engineering. The technical terms didn't make much sense at first, but I kept reading until I understood. I was on my way.

That was the great thing about electronics. I read about it, and practiced what I read, and got better. January's insoluble mysteries became child's play in March. By concentrating and studying, I could unravel any technical problem at all. At least that's how it felt. People problems . . . they were a whole 'nother matter. No matter how much we talked about girls, I never did figure them out.

I sure wanted a girlfriend, but I went with what I knew and where I found success. I may have been lonely, but electronics would soon give me my first real adult success. The complicated and frightening world of girls would have to wait. Meanwhile, I was absorbed, totally lost in the world of music, sound, and engineering.

Managing Sensory Overload

I grew up in a world of sensory overload. Every sound was like a fire alarm. The labels on my clothes clawed at me. Bright lights startled and blinded me. And the worst part was that no one seemed to believe me. Noise? What noise?

Part of the problem was that I could make noise or flash lights as loud or bright as I wanted, with no problems. As long as I was in control, my own light and sound never bothered me. I could shriek at the top of my lungs all day and feel fine, while everyone within a hundred yards wanted to throttle me. But if someone else made half that noise or flashed a light at *me*, I went nuts. Those dichotomies made people think I was just a spoiled brat. "He can dish it out fine, but he can't take it" was what my father said. If only they had understood.

When I was little, I had no way of knowing that I was more sensitive than other people. It would have amazed me to hear that something that was downright painful for me could go totally unnoticed by someone else. But that's the way it was. And when the grown-ups didn't notice what was bothering me, they tended to look at me like I was nuts, because I was getting uncomfortable and acting strange.

"He's a very sensitive little boy" was how my mother defended me. "He needs to toughen up" was my father's unsympathetic answer. And you know what? That's exactly what I did. I grew up to install sound systems and strobe lights in dance clubs and play rock and roll with some of the loudest bands on the planet. How did I go from extreme sensitivity to that level of tolerance?

How did I go from extreme sensitivity to that level of tolerance?

At a young age, I was fortunate to stumble upon special interests that captivated me and put my unique sensitivities to use in productive ways, opening a path out of disability. If all my brainpower was aimed at figuring out how a guitar amplifer or a Getrag* gearbox worked, those annoying thoughts and itchy tags could not get a word in edgewise. Without that Aspergian focus, and my aptitude for machines and electronics, my mind might well have been captured by all those stray sensory inputs that tormented me as a kid, and who knows where I might have ended up?

---

* Getrag is a German manufacturer of automobile gearboxes, or transmissions.

I wasn't always able to explain clearly how I managed to control my sensory overload. It wasn't until later in life that I was able to articulate the secret to my success.

I remember working on the sound crew at an Iron Butterfly concert shortly after the band got together for the second time. I was eighteen years old. We were playing in a big nightclub, not an arena. The place was packed, the ceiling was low, and the air was full of cigarette smoke. There was a projector throwing psychedelic images on the wall behind the stage, and the noise was blasting through the speakers. It was just the sort of place that could overwhelm anyone's senses.

When I recall those 1970s concerts, what I remember most are the patterns: the thumping melody of the bass, the dance of the VU meters on the amplifers, the smells of the hot vacuum tubes. I've never forgotten the silhouettes the spotlights cut through the smoke as I looked forward into the lights from behind the stage. The lights would hit the musicians' faces, and from where I stood, their hair would light up as if their heads had burst into flames.

What I don't remember is ever being troubled by the noise at those shows. When I learned about autism and about how many people, like me, have big issues with noises, I began to wonder, *How did I get away with that?*

The answer hit me last year, out of the blue, at a fundraising event for football star Doug Flutie's autism foundation.

Every winter, Doug organizes a bowling tournament to raise money for his foundation. His Flutie Bowls (as they are called) are always a good time, with catered food, music, and interesting people.

That year's bowl was held at a place called Jillian's in Boston. Jillian's is an old New England factory building that's been turned into an upscale bowling alley they call Lucky Strike Lanes. Doug gets so many people at his events that the crowd spills over onto the lower floors of Jillian's. But most of the action stays on the top floor, at Lucky Strike. That's where I was.

Up there, the bouncers string a velvet rope around the lanes to make a sort of VIP area. It quickly fills up with sponsors and sports figures who come to support Doug's foundation. When the night gets going, the VIP area is the only part of the establishment that isn't packed shoulder to shoulder. It's the equivalent of the backstage area at a sold-out rock concert. Fortunately, the foundation folks had given me a pass so I could escape to its relative calm and tranquillity.

I was very uncomfortable at first because I couldn't make sense of anything around me. Everywhere I looked there were people jostling, shoving, and shouting. There was no calm space in the alley. The whole room was packed with glittering socialites, hulking sports figures, and professional and amateur paparazzi snapping pictures. It was total sensory overload. You didn't have to be autistic to be freaked out in a madhouse like that.

Still, a fellow has to eat. I decided to wade into the crowd in search of food, which was visible above the sea of people, far across the room. I turned sideways, shoulder forward, and entered the crowd. The closer I got, the better the food smelled, which was good because the crush of people was almost enough to send me running for the exit. But I persevered, and eventually I reached the food tables. (Doug must be a well-respected figure in the Boston food service community, because the assortment of donated edibles was truly remarkable.)

A few minutes later, fortified by crab cakes, chocolate-covered strawberries, scallops, pizza slices, and small sweet pastries, I waded back past the velvet rope and made my way by the two burly bouncers to the VIP section.

There were supposedly many sports superstars in attendance, so I decided to see if I could pick them out. The crowd contained Patriots, Red Sox, and Celtics, but they all looked like regular people to me. I couldn't identify any of the pros in the group.

Failing in that effort, I looked out from the relative serenity of the VIP section. I decided to count girls to ascertain the male-to-female ratio of the crowd. What I found—sixteen girls for every ten guys—gave us males good odds that night. I counted another group of thirty people, just to be sure, and the ratio remained the same.

Then someone told me that I was expected to participate in the bowling competition. Turning my mind to the game at hand for a while, I discovered I wasn't half bad and actually scored a few strikes.

Having searched for sports figures, counted girls, and tried bowling, I was running out of things to do, so I decided to wander to the food again. As soon as I left the safety of the velvet rope, my anxiety returned. Feeling it, I started thinking I should slink out the door and head for home, but Doug saw me and said, "Wait a few minutes. My band is going to play soon."

I milled around, anxious and fidgety, looking for some distraction. Luckily, Doug's band chose that moment to start playing. I immediately walked to the rear of the bandstand and began listening. I focused on one instrument at a time, as I used to do back in my music-production days. After a moment I realized my anxiety had vanished. The beat of the music gave my mind something to lock on to. With that focus, I ceased to perseverate and worry.

> *I focused on one instrument at a time, as I used to do back in my music-production days. After a moment I realized my anxiety had vanished.*

Just then, I had a flash of insight. At Doug's event, of all places, I found the answer to why, at concerts, my sensory overload didn't kick in.

When Doug's band was playing I focused on different instruments one by one, as I had done years ago. It takes quite a bit of concentration to follow a single instrument, but I can do it.

People tell me that's an unusual ability, to be able to switch from one instrument to another at will, but those same people seem perfectly at ease in crowds or noisy places that freak me out, so perhaps it's a trade of one trait for the other. Maybe it's another Asperger job skill, one I share with every good music producer or orchestra conductor. A good many of them have Asperger's, too.

Other people on the spectrum may be different, but for me, the answer to handling crowds, noise, or flashing lights seems to be focus. If my mind is locked onto a target, it's as if all the distractions vanish. If I lose the target—whether it's a person I am tracking for a photo or a musician I am tracking for the sound—the sensory input overwhelms me. When I'm locked on, nothing bothers me. I learned that skill unconsciously when I was young, but now that I'm aware of it, I am able to adjust some of my life circumstances to make things go even more smoothly.

That's why I never attend concerts where I'm not working. In the audience I am constrained, and I have nothing to do, so I freak out, just as I was starting to do at the Flutie Bowl. I don't enjoy it, even today. For the same reason, I can't be alone in a crowded bar. If I have someone to focus on or a book to read, I can ignore the bedlam around me. Take that away, though, and I will be out the door and down the road in two minutes flat. Now that I understand what's happening, I am able to arrange things to avoid situations like that, and if people wonder why I don't do certain things, I have a good answer.

It seems like my "focus strategy" applies to sensory overloads of all sorts. Earlier, I talked about how I used concentration and focus to overcome touch sensitivity. So focus helps me with touch, noise, and probably a whole host of other issues. That may be because I have a greater-than-normal power of concentration, something that's pretty common in Aspergians. For me, it's key to managing sensory overload. It's funny, because I developed the ability long ago, before I had any knowledge of autism or the underlying issues.

A Walk in the Woods

I have always loved being in the woods. One of my favorite activities involves putting on my backpack and walking five or ten miles along forest trails here in western Massachusetts. I've walked many sections of the Appalachian Trail and Vermont's Green Mountain trails, and I hope to cover even more this coming season. I probably feel more at peace in the woods than anywhere else.

> *I probably feel more at peace in the woods than anywhere else.*

Walking in the woods is calming and tranquil. I listen to the birds and the bears, and the wind in the trees. Squirrels and snakes flit through the brush. Deer graze and hawks dive-bomb unsuspecting rodents. There's nothing quite like the rush of a mountain stream, tumbling through a gorge or down a ravine. I love the fresh mountain air, the textures, and the smells. And best of all—it's good for me. Walking is great exercise, especially when you carry a thirty-pound back-pack.

Some people look to nature for the sound of silence, but the woods where I roam are seldom truly quiet for more than a moment. Those moments—when they come—are magical. But when the woods go quiet for long seconds and you feel an unseen presence . . . watch out! It usually means some big predator is moving into the area, slow and quiet. Stealthy and hungry. Ready for action. That's the time to remember that humans are not always the top of the food chain, especially when you get far into the wild.

But I didn't start out in the wild. I started in some kinder, gentler woods behind my parents' home in Hadley, Massachusetts, just minutes from the busy UMass campus.

We moved to Hadley when I was eight, and I immediately headed for the hills. I never looked back. I can still remember how it felt to climb the high cliffs on Mount Holyoke, which towered above our house, less than a quarter mile away. The fear I felt when I got lost up there one dark night is still sharp and clear, but the memory of fun is even clearer. The neighbors' kids and I would hunt for amethyst crystals in the loose rock on the hillsides, and we imagined ourselves collecting priceless gemstones.

Yet some people hear about my love of the outdoors and they look at me like I'm crazy. My brother is a good example. "There are things out there that use trees for back scratchers, John Elder. I shine my flashlight into the woods at night and eyes reflect back at me. From eight feet off the ground!" Needless to say, my brother does not venture out to find the real answer—that those eyes belong to squirrels whose eyes glow as they sit on low-hanging tree branches.

What else can I do but feed his fears by agreeing? "Those are pine demons," I say with a serious expression. "Fierce fighters." Nothing more needs to be said. He remains in his house with windows closed and doors locked. I live next door, but I haven't even seen him in six months. Meanwhile, squirrels remain the unsung heroes of the rodent world.

My brother and I are opposites in many ways. He sees vicious predators at the border of his suburban lawn. I see even worse in the alleyways of Chicago and Houston. In a sense, both of us are right. It's just a matter of where one is comfortable, and what you choose to fear, if anything.

I'm certainly aware of the dangers that lurk in the countryside, but I don't dwell on them or let them hold me back. I grew up around the woods as a kid, both at my parents' home in Massachusetts and at my grandparents' farm in Georgia. When I was a teenager, I even left home and lived outside for a while, becoming a feral child. So I've had a lot of experience being in the country. All that time, I was aware of possible dangers, but I never felt threatened. And my confidence was justified, because nothing ever ate me.

It's true there are dangerous things in the woods, and nature can be harsh and unforgiving. But there's also great beauty and a sense of freedom. For me, the joys far out-weigh the threats. My time outdoors has taught me to appreciate the natural environment around me, and now it's almost second nature to read the signals of the outdoor world. I'm aware of changing weather, conditions under-foot, and wildlife around me. I sense all those things with-out really thinking, in the same way nypicals read the people around them at a party.

I can tell the call of a coyote from that of a bob-cat, and I know the feel of the changing air pressure just before the storm. I may be blind to the unspoken signals of other humans, but I read the messages of the natural world with a clarity few nypicals can muster.

> *I'm aware of changing weather, conditions under-foot, and wildlife around me. I sense all those things without really thinking, in the same way nypicals read the people around them at a party.*

I'm comfortable because the signals of the natural world are logical and un-emotional. They don't try to trick or deceive me. In some cases animals can be tricky, but their motivations are far simpler than those of most humans, and they are seldom nasty or mean, at least to me. I've pondered why it is that I have succeeded at learning to read the natural world, while I am still largely oblivious to the social cues of people. I think it comes down to simplicity, predictability, and logic. The natural world has all those things; people don't.

That's why, as hard as I've tried, I've never been truly comfortable at parties with groups of strangers. Yet I am completely comfortable walking up a strange hillside, even when the weather has changed and darkness falls. I've always felt secure and confident in the woods—two things I never feel at a party.

Given that reality, it's no surprise that I prefer nature to people. Some of the time. A wild animal won't act like your friend and then turn on you. Domestic animals don't behave that way, either. That's a uniquely human trait. The danger from animals is predictable and foreseeable. The same is true of other hazards in nature. An ice storm can kill you, but it's something anyone can anticipate, and most of all, storms are not malicious. People often are.

Over the years, many people have accompanied me on walks. Some companions have told me how safe they feel with me in the wilderness. Why would they say such a thing? When I ask, people say something like, "I'd be afraid to be out here by myself. But you seem to know what you're doing. You notice stuff."

For many years I listened to those remarks without giving them a second thought. But when I learned about Asperger's, and I learned about those weak mirror neurons that don't read feelings from other people very well . . . I started to wonder. Could they be doing something totally different in me? Is it possible that some part of my brain is attuned to subtle signals from the natural world, in a way that the brains of most other people aren't? And if that's true, is it an autistic thing or just a peculiarity of me? I don't know.

Temple Grandin may have alluded to something similar when she suggested that people with autism have more in common with animals than nypicals do, when it comes to how we see the world.

When I set out to write this chapter, my original point was that a walk in the woods allows me to unwind from the stress of dealing with other people. I still think that's true, but my unwinding happens in a place where there are even more true threats than the environment I'm escaping from. If I wanted "safe" relaxation, I'd be better off getting it at the local swimming pool, or on a treadmill in the security of my own home.

If you find a place where you can relax and unwind, you should treasure it and use it.

It's always stressful, trying to unravel the complex signals from other humans. Being in a crowd always tires me out for that reason. When I'm in the woods, I am free of that stressor. But I don't think that's the whole explanation for why being there feels better. Maybe it's a combination of things: the lack of people, the tranquillity of nature, and its natural beauty. Maybe outdoors is simply a place where I feel safer, and that's why I can unwind in a place where many people would feel alone and scared.

All of us need places where we feel safe. For some of us, it's in a small space, while others find solace in the wide-open outdoors. If you find a place where you can relax and unwind, you should treasure it and use it. I use nature to relax when I'm stressed and I just can't deal with humans anymore, or I'm tired of trying to figure out their motivations. I hope you have a place just like that.

A Day at the Races

I love the races at the Three County Fair. I've gone to the fair every Labor Day weekend for over thirty years. First my parents took me, and when I got big enough to drive, I took myself. It's irresistible. They've got rides, games, food, and agricultural exhibits. There are local people, city slickers, and sharp carnies and lowlifes looking to fleece us all. I used to try the rides and play the games, but now that I'm older, I head straight for the real action—the racetrack.

Many of my friends poke fun at my love of the fair and racing because they can't see what I see there, and they don't feel the track the way I do. If they did, they'd be right there beside me, waiting for the first race to start.

I always arrive early so I can secure a seat right against the fence rails, at the end of the long straightaway. That's the best place to be. During the race the champions thunder toward you full tilt, clods of dirt flying in their wake. As they struggle to make the turn in front, some of them will bounce off the railings and mix it up with the other racers. You can really feel the power of those beasts when you get that close. I like that.

As soon as I get there, I look for a nice grassy spot, one where I can see the action without getting trampled myself. I want to see the whole straightaway, but be partway into the turn. I prefer to sit on grass, but if I have to, I'll take hard-packed dirt. And I'm very particular about one thing: I won't sit anywhere that I see cigarette butts, trash, or spilled and rotting food. I also stay away from mystery liquid spots.

At a more upscale track those vile things would be easy to avoid, but this is the country, where all we have is dirt or grass. By the third day of a big fair, I have to do some hard and careful searching to find an acceptable place to sit.

> *You can really feel the power of those beasts when you get that close. I like that.*

I settle in and start to daydream. Sometimes I imagine the big tractors used to groom the fields at the fair plowing under all the trash that surrounds me. Next spring, a field of popcorn and cotton candy bushes would sprout, with the occasional funnel cake tree.

My daydreams are interrupted by the race caller, or talker. The talker is a carnie with a particularly loud and obnoxious voice who is able to talk reallyreallyreallyfast. His first job is to get the crowd going before every race, and he describes the action unfolding on the track for the benefit of any blind people in the crowd. He does it loudly enough so that the deaf know what's going on, too, and people with good hearing leave some of it at the end of the day.

Race callers have a long and sordid history. It all started with the invention of electronics to amplify the human voice to extraordinary levels, and loudspeakers to deliver the blast. By the mid-1920s, every track in the country wanted its own sound system, and a talker to go with it.

One of the most famous early talkers was Clem Mc-Carthy. According to David Halberstam's book *Sports on New York Radio,* McCarthy was hired in 1927 as the first track announcer in the country. He worked at Arlington Park in Arlington Heights, Illinois. That was the first track in the country to get a high-powered PA system and a talker to use it. The system worked so well that the Arlington Park track is still in business today. The sound system is updated, but the talker's routine is just the same as it was in the beginning, eighty years ago.

A good talker can work the crowd up something fierce. When that happens, the lines form at the betting window and the track owners smile. That's when they make their money. They take a small percentage of every bet, win, lose, or draw, and when millions are wagered their take can be substantial. Northampton doesn't have betting windows anymore, though, so I have to lay my bets among the race fans and bookies around me. It's more direct, and best of all, I don't pay a cut to the track.

Finally they're in the gate, ready to run the race. The talker has worked himself to a fever pitch, and all the bets are down. It's gotten really raucous, and I'm totally surrounded by people.. What a hodgepodge of humanity! There are couples on dates, with the guys trying to look cool and impress their girls with their suave knowledge of the track. Flitting through their midst are countless kids, like human flies, with parents trying to catch or ride herd over them. Farther back there's a group of hard-looking farmers: serious gamblers with fists full of cash and mouths full of chewing tobacco. In any other place I'd freak out in a crowded situation like this. But my Aspergian focus saves me. I'm concentrating so hard on the track that I don't even see the other people. I lean forward as I wait for the starting bell.

"And they're off!" The talker's shout is almost lost in the general bedlam and the sound of the bell, but then he finds his voice, and it soars over the noise of the crowd. "Here we go again, ladies and gentlemen! Pig Magic has the lead, but wait! Arnold Schwarzenpigger is coming up fast! And now Pigzilla is moving up! What's this action in the turn? Pigzilla has gone wild! He's just trampled Miss Piggy and he's closing in on the lead. Folks, that is some fast-moving bacon out there today!"

When you're down low you first feel the pounding of the hooves and then you see them coming toward the turn. You can look them dead in the eye as they barrel down the straightaway, racing right toward you, just as fast as they can. Just as you're sure you're about to be trampled they lean hard, dirt flies, and they're into the turn and past. The ground shakes from the pounding of hooves, and I smell their hot breath. In just a moment they've come and gone, with nothing left but the breeze and the smells and a few bits of grass and dirt swirling in their wake. *These pigs really do fly,* I say to myself.

I'm glad they're not chasing me through a field, bent on destruction. (I had some experiences like that as a kid, back on the farm in Georgia. I'm happy to have a good fence between me and them.)

When you're down low you first feel the pounding of the hooves and then you see them coming toward the turn.

Every noise is a shout. The talker is yelling, and the crowd yells back. A kid in a blue shirt about ten feet from me yells loudest of all, after he stuck his hand through the rail with a Butterfinger bar, and Pig Mania bit his thumb off. Didn't he see the sign: WARNING—THESE PIGS BITE! And that's not all . . . they're biting each other! "What's that?" The talker picks up the chant. "Pigzilla has just bitten Pig Magic and she's off like a shot! Pig Magic has the lead! It's Pig Magic ahead by a nose. Now he's ahead by a pork barrel and they're on the final stretch. Pig Magic has it! We have a winner! Piiiiiiiiiig *Magic!*" After stretching the "Pig" part, "Magic" comes out like the crack of a whip, and it's all over.

My ears are ringing, but I'm wearing a big smile because I'm up fifty bucks on a long-shot bet. Back in the crowd, there are smiles and frowns as piles of money are pushed across tables between furtive-looking men. Farm boys spit their tobacco, and small children wipe vile brown wads from their shirts as they look around in puzzlement. The alkies sip from brown-bagged bottles as medics tend to the foolish kid that lost his thumb. *Next time,* I say to myself, *he'll read the warning signs.* Children run through the thinning crowd, pulling up clumps of grass and tossing them. Mothers chase them, and the scene devolves until it's time for the next race.

I really love a good pig race. There's nothing to match it at the county fair, except maybe the mud wrestling or the demolition derby. Some people read my accounts of events like this and say, "You sure live in a different world from mine. I've gone to that fair all my life and I've never seen anything like you describe."

It's not my fault that you didn't see it. Just be glad I did, and consider it as one more example of how we Aspergians see the world in a wholly unique light. Where would society be without people like me to bring stories like these to the public's attention? And if you see the fair the same way I do, congratulate yourself on being a fellow freak. There's an open cage just waiting for you, out back behind the pig track.

> *Where would society be without people like me to bring stories like these to the public's attention?*

Part 5

Finding Your Gifts

In the previous chapters I've done my best to show you the *why* behind my own, sometimes strange, behavior. I hope that in doing so I've shed some light on your own behaviors and those of the people around you.

There is more than one way to approach almost any problem. You can cut a tree down with an ax, a chain saw, a bulldozer, or a heavy machine gun. The path we choose is influenced by who we are and our environment. The more different you are from other people, the more likely you are to solve problems in a unique way. That may be a handicap in school, where they expect you to do things the teacher's way. Once you get out of school, though, your difference can become a powerful competitive advantage.

In this last section, I've tried to summarize some of the things I've done to take my knowledge of Asperger's and my insight into my own behavior and forge them into a successful package. I hope you'll be able to do the same.

Learning Calculus

One of the first signs that electronics had taken over my life was the change in my room. Winnie the Pooh bedspreads and bright curtains were gone, replaced by test equipment, tools, and vacuum tubes. My bedroom had become a lab. Parental influence was nowhere to be seen.

My grandparents had given me a huge Fender Showman guitar amplifier, which filled one corner of my room. Another corner had shelves of components. (They were very special shelves. I had made them myself in Mr. Jacque's woodshop class.) On the other side of my room, I'd converted my dresser top to a workbench, though "converted" may be too strong a word. Perhaps it would be more accurate to say, *I drilled holes and cut bits from the top of my dresser while using it as a workbench*. My bed was next to that, but you couldn't see it because it was hidden beneath a pile of filthy clothes, sheets, and blankets. The carpet underfoot was sharp with little snippets of wire and clipped lead wires from resistors and capacitors.

I lurked in the midst of it all, staring into the round screen of my oscilloscope. I'd sit watching and listening for hours, absorbing music and unraveling how sound waves looked and how electrical signals worked.

The whole process had started the year before, when I discovered the oscilloscope. In fact, a lot of people don't even know what an oscilloscope is, so I'll take a moment to tell you. The oscilloscope is a device that displays electrical signals as lines and shapes on a small screen. It allowed me to see the music I loved as patterns on the screen, patterns that I could unravel to gain a deeper understanding of how things worked. You may not believe that geeky piece of electronic test gear could be life-changing, but it sure was for me.

You may not believe that geeky piece of electronic test gear could be life-changing, but it sure was for me.

I was drawn to those squiggly lines from the moment I saw them. Each signal had its own unique shape when viewed on the oscilloscope. The constant voltage from a battery made a flat line. It didn't change over time. The signals on the phone line were a whole different story, though. They were alive and dynamic when seen on the scope. The dial tone appeared as a smooth wave pattern, while a honking busy signal made a more complex image. And a conversation was the most complex signal of all.

There were oscilloscopes in the electronics classroom

at the high school, but the best scopes were in the audio-
visual repair department or in the engineering labs at the
university, so that's where I spent all my time in the beginning. Later, when I got a scope of my own, I became
self-sufficient. I was able to look at patterns eight or ten
hours a day, and that's what I did, just about every day.

Those green lines on the screen opened up a whole new
world for me. The concept of seeing sound seemed magical, yet I understood what I was seeing—it all made sense.
Watching sounds on that scope was even better than *Lost in
Space* or any other TV show. I watched and listened and
watched some more until my eyes and ears became inter-
changeable. By then, I could look at a pattern on the scope
and know what it sounded like, and I could listen to a
sound and know what it looked like.

Music was the thing that gave meaning to all of this.

I learned to adjust the scope to reveal its different parts.
If I set the scope to sweep slowly, the rhythm of the music
dominated the screen. Loud passages would appear as
broad streaks, while quiet passages thinned down to a single
tiny squiggle. A slightly higher sweep speed showed me
the big, heavy, slow waves of the bass line and the kick
drum as wide squiggles. Most of the energy was contained
in those low notes. Up higher, with a faster scope setting,
I found the vocals. At the top of it all lay the jagged fast
waves from the cymbals.

Every instrument had a distinct pattern, even when
they were all playing the same melody. With practice, I
learned how to distinguish a passage played on an organ

from the same music played on a guitar. But I didn't stop there. As I listened to the instruments, I realized that each one had its own voice. "You're nuts," my friends said, but I was right. The musicians all had their own ways of playing, but their instruments were unique, too. Actually, it was the musicians who taught me to tell them apart.

With practice, I learned how to distinguish a passage played on an organ from the same music played on a guitar.

"Just listen to that guy play," they'd say. Often they'd be talking about the musician and his style, like Alvin Lee of Ten Years After or B. B. King playing the blues. But other times they talked about the sound, and they jumped on me fast if I failed to pick up the difference. "You're not paying attention, man," they would say. "Just listen to that guitar. Can't you hear that hollow-body Gibson sound?" When I got it right, the older musicians praised me. "That kid is smarter than any houseplant," they said, and I wriggled my ears in appreciation.

With a lot of practice I got the ability to listen to a song and say, "He's playing a Fender Precision bass" or "That keyboard player has a Hammond and a Korg." Before you conclude that that ability is rare, let me put it in perspective. There were musicians who taught me who could go beyond simply identifying a Fender Precision bass. They could pick a particular Precision by its unique tone qualities, and they could tell one Precision from another when listening to a recording. "This is an old pre-CBS Fender," I'd hear. "They always sound the best." Sometimes they told me what kind of strings the instrument was strung with, and when I checked, they were always right.

That same ability must have been latent in me, because the more deeply I immersed myself in music, the better I became, and soon I was just as confident of my musical insight as any professional musician. I wonder if anyone can do this but most people never know, or if this is a rare gift I have.

People have asked me what the secret was to the way I could resolve such fine details in sound, but I don't think there was one. It just took a good dose of concentration, some motivation, and a few thousand hours of looking and listening, and there I had it. I built my musical insight the way you'd build a stone wall . . . one note or one stone at a time, with a lot of dedication and persistence. My ability to focus surely helped, but most of my ability came about through countless hours of hard work. It feels strange to think of listening to music as practice or training, but that's what it was for me. And I added an additional sensory input: I watched.

The scope patterns helped me learn what set the instruments apart. The secret was all in the harmonics, the components sound waves are built from. I was able to see them on the scope, but it took all those hours to unravel the way visual patterns related to the design subtleties of musical instruments and circuits.

My ability to recognize the voices of the individual instruments took me much deeper into the music. If I listened to a song and recognized a Rickenbacker bass, I could see it in my mind, just as I could see every other instrument being played. It was almost like being there. The music came steadily more alive as my insight deepened.

The most complex patterns emerged when different instruments played together. At first, they were hard to unravel with my ears and virtually impossible to sort out with my eyes. But I persisted. At times, the screen could just dissolve into a blur of light, until I taught myself how to adjust the scope to emphasize different components of the sound. With practice, I was beginning to decode the secrets of music, and with it, waveform mathematics.

> *I was beginning to decode the secrets of music, and with it, waveform mathematics.*

I didn't even see it as math. I saw the whole thing as a great mental puzzle— adding the waves from different instruments in my head, and figuring out what the result would look like. The biggest challenge was learning how the different shapes I saw in my mind actually sounded. With practice, I became pretty good at it, and my imagination began matching reality. As my knowledge expanded, I began asking bigger questions. How do electronic circuits alter sounds? I know what an echo sounds like, but what does it look like? How are special effects created?

I started building simple circuits and looking at how they altered the wave patterns. For example, I learned how a fuzz box made the honking guitar sound on the Beatles' "Revolution." I learned about the effect they call flanging on songs like Orleans's "Love Takes Time." Once I saw them and heard them, I understood their workings. I always asked myself, *What's next?* I built new circuits, and predicted how my changes would look and sound. I was thrilled when I was right and puzzled when I wasn't.

Those circuits were hard to figure out at first. I'll bet I spent two hundred hours wrestling with my first audio amplifier. There were days when I almost cried with frustration, and my wall had dents where I punched it in anger as I struggled to make things work. But I got faster as I got more experience. Soon my designs began working, right off the drawing board.

I wish there were a secret to share for my eventual success, but there isn't. I just solved one puzzle after another. Some took me forward in huge steps, while other discoveries showed me the error of a previous "breakthrough." If there is a secret to that at all, it's probably that I was too pigheaded and stubborn to quit.

I never had a shortage of ideas, and within a few years I developed a solid enough foundation of knowledge to think of something new and turn the concept to reality fairly successfully.

By then, I had gone from unraveling other people's devices to inventing my own. That was what took me to the top in music. Rock-and-roll musicians always wanted something unique. Companies popped up every day, selling little special-effects boxes that changed the sound of an instrument. There were phasers, doublers, wah-wah, distortion, echo, and reverb. The list was endless. I began building my own devices, but instead of putting them in boxes, I built them right into the instruments. I also built effects that became part of the main sound system. It was a wonderful, creative time for me. I had truly found the first of my Aspergian gifts.

I'd imagine a wave from a musical instrument, feed it into a circuit in my mind, and look and listen to the result. If I liked what I heard, I built the circuit and fine-tuned it. If it didn't work, I thought of something else that did. When my own thoughts weren't enough, I turned to books with titles like *Active Filter Design* and *Signal Processing Electronics*. That's where I sometimes ran into trouble.

The books were filled with formulas, which I did not understand. I looked at the symbols and equations on the pages and got nothing. But I looked at the schematic drawings—the circuit layouts—and things began to make sense. I'd stare at a circuit and imagine a simple wave. I'd put the wave into the circuit and imagine the result. I'd read the descriptions and compare those to the patterns in my mind.

Looking back at that time, I now see what was happening. I didn't relate to math symbols, but I had taught myself to "read" a circuit diagram the way most mathematicians solve equations. Electronic components had taken the place of mathematical symbols for me. I couldn't make any sense of an integral signal and some formula in a calculus book. But I knew exactly what happened when I connected resistors, capacitors, and amplifiers to integrate a signal in real life. The thing was, the calculus concept of integration was a meaningless abstract. Reality for me was the way I added harmonics to a simple wave to turn it from a curve to a sawtooth shape. And I knew how that changed the sound, making it smooth and fat.

Ultimately, sound was what mattered. The equations on the page were just dry representations of the sounds I created by applying my vision and imagination. The sound was what was real. That's the same thing other inventors have realized since the beginning of time.

A math professor called me out on that one day. He said, "How can you say you understand calculus concepts

> *I couldn't make any sense of an integral signal and some formula in a calculus book. But I knew exactly what happened when I connected resistors, capacitors, and amplifiers to integrate a signal in real life.*

if you can't even pass algebra?" Years ago, I was demeaned by comments like that, but today I understand the answer.

Modern math teachers say Isaac Newton invented calculus in the seventeenth century. The implication of that statement is that advanced math did not exist before that day. That's not true. Math is merely a set of tools to represent complex things that have always happened in the real world. If you can see into the patterns of nature, like the movements of the planets or the interplay of musical notes to make a melody . . . you are seeing the foundation that modern representational math was built upon. That's a fairly uncommon ability that I now know to be a gift of my Asperger's.

We've developed the written mathematics to describe the movement of the sun and stars only in the last few hundred years, but the Mayans and Egyptians somehow figured out many of those same things a thousand or more years ago. You can find examples of inventors and engineers with instinctive insights into complex problems throughout history. Perhaps they were Aspergians, too.

My ability to twist and shape waves in my mind may not be as precise as a mathematician with a computer, but for my purposes, that didn't matter. My imagination was close enough to reality that I could hit my target by thinking of a circuit, building it, and refining it through a bit of experimentation. There are lots of people out there who know calculus. The number of people who grasp its principles intuitively and use them to invent things is a lot smaller. I didn't know that then, but there was never any reason for me to feel inferior to other engineers, despite what people said.

By arranging different components in my mind I could make a saxophone solo sound like the instrument took wing and flew. I could put some bottom under the organ, so the bass notes sounded like distant rolling thunder. I'd make the drums snap in that unique way that got the audience clapping along with the band. I heard those things first in my head. Then I made them real when I built my designs.

If you asked a mathematician what I did, he'd describe extremely complex calculus functions that transformed one wave pattern into another. He'd write symbols and equations that only a math professor would understand. Looking at them on a paper, they wouldn't mean a thing to me. They'd be just as flat and lifeless as the sheet they were written on. I could never make any sense of them.

To me, the waves were like living things. They went into imaginary circuit components in my mind, and they emerged transformed. I could bend and shape them,

> *To me, the waves were like living things.*

and view them from any angle. My resistors, capacitors, and other imaginary parts took the place of math symbols in my head. The shapes they made became sounds in my imagination. That's why I never learned traditional math. I left it behind with my mathematical vision. And it worked.

When I think of earlier inventors, I realize that many of them must have had a similar intuitive understanding of higher mathematics. I now know that it's possible to add waves in your head, even if you can't write the formulas to do it on paper.

I'm with the Band

Lots of young people go to Hollywood, but very few become stars. Of all the high school bands, how many reach national prominence? With those odds, why would a logical guy like me ever choose a career in music, and how could someone as socially disabled as I am possibly succeed?

The obvious answer is that I created some things the world had never seen before. With their fire, light, and action, my special-effects guitars made the musical instrument a centerpiece of the rock-and-roll show, and set the stage for countless effects that followed, in movies, on MTV, and in today's music videos. The equipment I built for Pink Floyd's sound company delivered powerful music to countless people at concerts all over North America, and that paved the way for the sophisticated digital concert sound systems in use today.

Stated that way, my accomplishments sound awfully grand. In reality, what I did was quite a bit simpler, and more attainable. If I had to describe my abilities I'd say I was first a circuit designer, a person who invented an electronic circuit to solve a particular problem. It just so happens that my particular skill was really evident because I used it to create things the whole world could see or hear. Other designers might well have been more talented than I was, but the area where they worked was obscure. For example, another engineer I know invented a brilliant method of regulating the throttle in a car, but no one outside the car industry ever noticed his creative genius. That's still true today, even though millions of cars now drive around on his inventions. You might say electronic design was my "core skill," and that skill was certainly facilitated in a big way by my Aspergian brain differences.

> *I was a loner when it came to creating my designs, but I was a team player when it came to building them.*

The second "success skill" is that I was a loner when it came to creating my designs, but I was a team player when it came to building them. For example, I envisioned the light guitar that Ace Frehley made famous, but my abilities stopped at thinking up the concept and designing the circuits. I turned to Jim Boughton to engineer and make the structure of the thing, and my girlfriend Little Bear for all the actual electronic assembly. When the "light guitar" part was done, I took my creation to Long Island luthier Steve Carr, who worked the frets and action to make a guitar you could actually play, and play well. I could never have made that instrument without those people. The same was true for most of my other creations—I relied on others to help carry my ideas to completion.

So was I just a cog in the machine? Surely, I was more than that. First, I had the vision followed by the drive to make things happen. Millions of people see an unmet need and say, "Someone should invent an xyz. . . ." I am someone who's said that, and then actually followed through, many times in my life. I don't know what you call that trait, but it's not genius. Maybe it's imagination plus determination, or stubbornness, or something else. Whatever you call it, I know that many people today could go much further if they just took the next step, when they had an idea, instead of letting it die as idle conversation.

Then there's teamwork. We live in a complex world, one where it's nearly impossible for any one person to "do it all," no matter how smart he or she may be. When it came time for me to build the devices I'd imagined, I knew I could not do it alone. That capacity—the ability to know what you don't know, and know what you need—is vital to success. I assembled a little team and served as its leader of sorts.

Finally, there's self-confidence, and that's a funny thing. Most people think self-confidence relates to other people, and I have no confidence when it comes to intimate matters with others. When I was twenty-one, if you had pointed to a pretty girl and said, "Go say hi to MaryAnne; she thinks you're sweet," I would have been far too shy to budge. But if you had said, "Can you design a guitar that would project a laser show back over the audience?" I would have said, "Sure, why not?" And I would have started thinking, and spouting ideas, and in minutes I'd have been far down the road to a laser guitar light show.

I think that's an Asperger thing. My social disability kept me miles away from MaryAnne, whatever she may have thought. Yet when I turned to machines instead of people, I had great success, and I knew it, and that made me confident in that arena. Finally, my concentration and focus let me dive into the light show in ways that ordinary people simply couldn't.

My concentration and focus let me dive into the light show in ways that ordinary people simply couldn't.

Why music at all? Why not rocketry, or psychology, or chemical engineering? The simple answer is, those things didn't really interest me. In addition, there was the reality of my situation, when I started my work life at age sixteen. People who look at my life today often assume I chose music from the whole universe of careers that exist. That's not accurate. I didn't choose to be a high school dropout; I became one when I could not (or would not) do the work my teachers set in front of me. Dropping out pretty much limited my career options to the trades (being a plumber or car mechanic), low-income service work (changing bedpans in a nursing home or waiting on tables), crime (stealing things or dealing drugs), or doing something weird (joining the circus or playing rock and roll).

None of those options seemed very good. I feel bad saying that today, with my adult perspective, because I've learned that you can have rewarding and successful careers in any of those areas. After all, I went on to have great success in life as a mechanic by founding Robison Service when I was about thirty years old. I know people who've done very well owning and running restaurants, nursing homes, junkyards, and even electrical contracting companies. Most of those folks—like me—came up through the ranks by learning their trade and then running the business. All of us are proof that you can make it outside the traditional college, white-collar-job career path; and doing so can leave you richer and more fulfilled than many bachelor's-degree-carrying drones.

However, all that knowledge was far in the future the day I found myself set free of school. At that moment, I could not see any sure or safe paths to success and happiness, so I chose the thing that sounded easiest and most fun . . . music.

Even then, I sensed that my ability to repair musical instrument electronics and fix and modify amplifiers was rare. At age sixteen, I could name a hundred local musicians, but I could not think of a single person who could do what I did, and who did it in music. You might say I found a niche and exploited it.

I saw that there were lots of musicians. I knew that most of them would never make it to the big time, but as long as they were on the journey, someone had to keep their amplifiers humming and their guitars playing. *Could that be me?* I wondered. *Why not?* Musicians did not care if I had a high school diploma, much less a college degree. They just cared how I made them sound. It was a results-oriented thing, pure and simple. That was ideal for me, because my endless electronic experimentation had made me into a results-oriented guy.

At the same time, I knew there were other people who could do what I did. Sort of. For example, there were Fred Smead, John Fuller, and Sam Skilling back in the AV Department at Amherst Regional High School. They all knew how to fix amplifiers, but did they care? Not really. Those guys had secure jobs keeping all the electronics of the Amherst School System humming. They had no need for a bunch of grungy musicians; they had steady paychecks from the school.

So the people who needed me (musicians) didn't know anyone else with skills like mine. The people with skills like mine (commercial electronics technicians) didn't care much about musicians. It was a perfect opportunity, and I made the most of it.

Finally, there was me, and my own differences. In the world of music, Asperger's did not disable me. In fact, my brain differences were really key to my success. How? you ask. I'll show you. . . .

My brain differences were really key to my success.

My lack of social skill isolated me from other people. That made me lonely, but it also gave me time to find other interests. While nypical kids were dating and partying, I studied circuits. By the time I was eighteen I'd invested so much time learning music and electronics that a nypical kid would be hard-pressed to ever catch me.

My Aspergian special interests and focus really kept me on target. While the nypical kids flitted from one interest to another, I stayed locked on my goals. From the time I turned thirteen, I pursued just two interests: music/electronics and transportation machinery. I've stayed on course with those interests ever since. I may not have had many friends, and I sure felt the hurt of being alone, but I was able to find solace and success by doing what I was really meant to do. Now, as a successful adult, I find myself making lots of new friends because people appreciate what I've done with machines, and I've come full circle. Today, I am on the verge of being popular.

When you're a kid, people make fun of your special interest. When you're a grown-up, though, your special interest makes you the expert—the go-to guy—for whatever it is you really love.

Plastic Brains

People often comment on the speed with which I can acquire new knowledge. When I was a kid grown-ups would tease me when they saw me reading books about ships or machinery, but they were always impressed with the technical details I remembered. I don't have a photographic memory, but I am pretty good at retaining the essence of whatever I read. I also remember things I see and do, which is a help whenever I have to find my way home from a strange place, or reassemble something I took apart.

"That's a wonderful gift," my grandmother would tell me. "You're such a smart little boy." I may not have known about Asperger's, but I knew I learned fast from an early age. I could see the difference between the speed with which I picked things up, and the struggles

> *I may not have known about Asperger's, but I knew I learned fast from an early age.*

of other kids in my class. I wish I could say that made me a top student, but it didn't. I may have known I was a better reader than Mikey Thomas, but he still plodded along and got As, while I flitted from one book to another and struggled for a C.

My problem with learning fast in school was simple. The scope of what the school gave me to do was too small. My teacher might say, "This weekend, I want you kids to read about the Louisiana Purchase on pages 60 to 73 of your American history book." I'd go home, get interested, and read the whole book. Somewhere inside, I'd find something a lot more interesting, and off I'd go on that tangent, leaving the original assignment behind. By Monday it was totally forgotten. Or even worse, I'd pick up the book, decide it was poorly written or wrong or boring, and simply move on to something else. None of those actions led to good grades, even though I acquired a lot of knowledge on the path to a C or a D.

Knowing that, I'll bet I could have done a lot better in school if I'd had a grown-up to keep me focused on the assignments. Someone who said, "Hold on, John. Let's do what the teacher asked before moving on to the history of California." I know some Asperger schools do that today, with great success.

My ability to acquire new skills may not have gotten me ahead in school, but it saved me after I dropped out.

When I was nineteen I decided I needed a regular job in addition to the work I'd been doing with local rock-and-roll bands since leaving school. I thought about what

I could do and settled on being a car mechanic. I'd never worked for any legitimate employer before, and I had no experience fixing cars other than working on my own and my friends', but I went for it anyway. A help-wanted ad for Don Lorenz GMC-Buick-Cadillac caught my eye. I didn't know much about GMC, but my grandfather always drove Cadillacs, and that's what I decided to become—a Cadillac mechanic. I got some copies of *Hot Rod* and *Motor Trend,* and reread the *Handbook of Automotive Technology* that my uncle had given me.

I studied for several days, and went to the job interview with my brain packed full of all the automotive knowledge I could fit. It worked. The service manager talked to me for about half an hour, concluding with "When can you start?" He went on to say I was the most literate-sounding person who had ever applied there, and one of the only ones who could fill out the job application legibly. I thanked my lucky stars for all those *quick brown fox jumps over the lazy dog* writing exercises in grammar school.

Within a few months I'd combined my love of cars and my fascination with electronics to turn myself into the dealership's resident auto electronics expert. I rebuilt alternators and starters, and solved wiring problems no one else could unravel. From an experience base of zero, I made myself into an above-average Cadillac mechanic, or at least a Cadillac electronics mechanic. I worked at Lorenz for two years before leaving to return to the music world full-time.

One of the keys to my success was that I became an expert in something no one else understood—automotive electronics. That happened to be a subset of auto mechanics where I could really shine. Other areas of mechanics required strength, fine coordination, and many hours of practice on a particular car—none of which I had. But when a Coupe de Ville blew a fuse every time you opened the passenger door, you did not need strength, long practice, or a steady and smooth hand to find the problem. You needed abstract reasoning skill. And it turned out I had that aplenty.

> *One of the keys to my success was that I became an expert in something no one else understood—automotive electronics.*

A few years later, I repeated that performance when I saw the chance to get a job as a digital engineer. Unfortunately, my only engineering experience was with analog circuits, and that wasn't traditional workplace experience—my designs were done on sheets of paper in all-night diners and prototyped in the basement of my house. But as luck would have it, I had something no other applicant had—experience designing sound systems. And that's what the job was about—designing talking toys and sound effects for Milton Bradley, the electronic game maker. So I got some books on digital design, studied hard, and less than two weeks later I presented myself as a digital

designer with audio experience. It would be tempting to
say I just bluffed my way into that job, and maybe I did, but
my boss always said I was one of his top engineers. So I
must have learned fast enough for him!

Once again, I combined a small amount of experience
and practical knowledge with my innate reasoning power,
and I succeeded. I used logic to unravel how something
worked, which added to my store of practical knowledge.
The first time I solved a problem, I started with a clean
slate, asking, *How does this function?* Each solution I figured
out added to my collection of mental shortcuts. Those
shortcuts then saved me time when I used them to build
new things or to attack similar problems. In that way, I
built a powerful technical capability rapidly and effectively.

Those are all examples of how I've used my autistic
brain plasticity to acquire new skills rapidly and use them
to get ahead. Autism has presented me with many challenges, but plasticity is truly one of my gifts.

Attention to Detail

I have always paid attention to the little things. My first ten-speed bike was a case in point. When my father took me to pick it up, I immediately turned it over and began studying the gears. "What's that?" I asked, pointing to the mechanism at the rear wheel. I saw SIMPLEX printed on the casting. "That's a derailleur," the bike man said. "It swings in and out to shift the chain from one gear to another. Watch." He pedaled the bike and moved the lever. I watched the chain move up the gears, and I was smitten.

I have always paid attention to the little things.

There was just one problem. I was troubled by the word "derailleur." When I heard it, the pronunciation was de-RAILer. Well, I knew what a derailer was, and it wasn't something on the back wheel of a bike. A real derailer is a device bolted to a railway track to derail a runaway train car before it crashes into something more important. But I decided to let his derailleur slide, because I was old enough to know that claiming greater knowledge often meant more trouble in dealings with strangers. Especially strangers with bogus French-sounding words on bikes.

Some boys my age had girlfriends. I had mechanical devices. Once I discovered bicycle gears, I had to know all about them. I went to Peloton—the bike store in my town—and stared through the glass at brand-new derailleur sets in boxes. I compared the different brands. Campagnolo was the best, and it showed. The whole assembly was made from beautifully finished aluminum alloy. My Simplex set was just plastic, a cheap toy by comparison. Then there was the Shimano, and a few others whose names I've forgotten.

I knew and loved them all. Whenever I passed a bicycle parked on the street, I had to stop and examine its hardware. Sometimes I even moved the levers to test the "feel" of the mechanisms. People made fun of my fascination with gears, but I knew that the people who designed racing bicycles were just as fascinated as I was. The only difference was, they were older and they had jobs. I was just a kid in school.

Some people would say my whole fascination with gears was weird. They'd say, "Most kids would be interested in riding the bike, not figuring out how its gears work." Maybe that's true. But for every hundred people who ride bikes, at least one designer and a few repairers will surely be needed. And who will they be, if not kids like me?

I ignored the kids who made fun of me and taught myself how bicycles worked. I taught myself to clean and adjust every single part. Each brand was different, but I learned them all. I taught myself how properly adjusted gears feel by placing my hands on the lever and the

> *For every hundred people who ride bikes, at least one designer and a few repairers will surely be needed. And who will they be, if not kids like me?*

mechanisms as I pedaled the bikes on my bench top. I have pretty sensitive touch, which allowed me to sense the condition of mechanical things through my hands. And the more I practiced, the better my ability to sense machinery became.

As I turned the pedals on an old bike I'd feel tiny bumps as grains of sand passed through the gears. If I cleaned the chain with an oiled rag, those little bumps would go away. But that wasn't all—I'd feel little grabs as I pedaled through tight spots, where the chain might not be properly oiled. I could even feel sloppiness when the crank bearings were too loose. I learned to feel every moving part of the bicycle with just a few simple touches. When I adjusted the derailleur mechanism I'd feel carefully to make sure the chain ran perfectly in both the top and bottom gears. With that ability, I could almost diagnose and adjust bikes blindfolded.

Other kids saw what I could do, and they started asking me to tune up their bikes. Somehow, bikes I adjusted didn't look any different, but they shifted better and rode smoother. It was a small triumph that gained me a measure of respect at school. I felt good about that, but pride wasn't all I got for my efforts. They also made me lunch money.

A few years later, I applied my mechanical talents to motorcycles instead of bikes, and had even more success. My friend Juke told me about an old Honda 150 Dream motorbike abandoned in a basement. After buying it for twenty-five dollars I turned it into a smooth-running machine that carried me all over New England. That motorcycle was what allowed me to escape the confines of Amherst High into the real world. As soon as I started riding my machines through the halls of the school, the administrators threw me out.

For the past twenty years, I've actually made a career of my love of machines. I founded a company—J E Robison Service—that specializes in difficult service on Land Rovers, Mercedes-Benzes, Rolls-Royces, BMWs, and other fine cars. I chose those makes because they have the best craftsmanship in the world, and they are owned by people who value what they have. It's turned out to be a good match.

My clients can see my love of their machinery, and they appreciate my talents. It's a grown-up version of the bicycle tinkering I did in high school. Cars are a lot more complex than bikes, but my skills have expanded to match. It's worked out well. My social skills may still be weak, but that's not what people look for when they bring me a Land Rover to have its rough-running engine repaired. They want craftsmanship, something a person like me can deliver in spades.

"How do you do it?" When I hear those words, I think what people are really asking is, "What do you do to achieve such a great result with my car? How are you different from other mechanics?"

There are several answers. The first is that I work with the machines I do because I have a real affinity for them.

Once I took an interest in them, I made it my business to know all things Rover. I took them apart and put them back together until I figured out how they worked. Today, I work around Land Rovers during the day. I write articles for Land Rover enthusiast magazines. I get in my Range Rover to drive home, and on the weekend my friend Dave and I pile into our Land Rover Defenders for some serious off-road driving. So I am immersed in the machinery that surrounds me.

There is a sharp contrast between people like me and mechanics who are just in the trade for money. They go to work at the Cadillac dealer, then climb into a Subaru when it's time to go. They don't "live" Cadillac. They don't immerse themselves in the machines like I do. My job is my love; his is a living.

The next component to my success is practice. The saying "Practice makes perfect" does hold true. I've seen thousands and thousands of Land Rovers, and I've handled every bit of every model. Cars are like people—they evolve and change with time. Every year there are new models and little changes, and I spend the time to stay current. Even existing Rovers change as owners fix and modify them. I know how Land Rovers feel, how they fail, and what to do to make each one sing. There is really no substitute for practice and the long easy familiarity that comes from it.

> *There is really no substitute for practice and the long easy familiarity that comes from it.*

The first two components of my success are within reach of anyone, Aspergian or nypical. The next secrets to my success are ways in which my Asperger's sets me apart and gives me key competitive advantages.

Like many with Asperger's, I have an extraordinary power of concentration. I can look into a mechanical system until it becomes my whole world. That hyperfocused concentration is a key to really understanding what's going on at an elemental level. It's an ability I used to take for granted—I assumed everyone could do it. Today I know it's a rare gift. People ridiculed me for being in my own world as a kid, but no one ridicules me as a grown-up tuning an antique engine.

My unusual concentration is buttressed by knowledge, and that in turn comes from what psychologists call the "special interests." As a kid, I was teased because when I got interested in something I talked about that topic, about trains or bugs or whatever else, until everyone around me was bored to tears. As a child, my thirst for knowledge about a few specific topics may have seemed strange. (And I'm sure my rants annoyed people around me.) But as an adult, that drive for knowledge helped me become an expert. Sure, I may go on and on about Land Rovers until you are about to scream from boredom, but isn't that the kind of person you'd choose to make your old Rover better than new?

And when I do make an adjustment or a repair to your car, it's done right or not at all. Sometimes I know it's perfect right away; other times I tinker and tinker and then go back to check it ten more times. It's just how I am. Before I learned about Asperger's, I just figured I was a fussy sort of guy. Now I know I can thank my Asperger's for my need to know everything possible about something, and to do my work as perfectly as I can. Just like stacking blocks back on the playground.

> *Now I know I can thank my Asperger's for my need to know everything possible about something, and to do my work as perfectly as I can.*

I sure wish I could have seen my future when people called me names as a kid. And it wasn't just the other kids—even teachers made fun of my focus and interests. It's ironic how that works. Even today, psychologists say special interests and extreme focus are abnormal in a teenager. But if the person is twenty-five, the same shrinks call him an expert. That's what happened to me.

The world really does get better for Aspergians, and indeed for all sorts of geeks and misfits, as we grow up.

Secrets of My Success

W hen I look back at the stories in this book, a few key insights come into focus. These are the highlights of what I have discovered while struggling as an Aspergian throughout my life, albeit unknowingly for the first forty years. I hope you've enjoyed reading about my experiences, and that you've learned some helpful tricks, hints, and techniques that you can apply to your own life. Here's what I suggest.

Find Your Strengths and Interests

The first secret is that you must figure out what you're good at and stick with it. In school a lot of emphasis is put on identifying your weaknesses and then improving them. That's important if your weaknesses are holding you back, but it's not the path to greatness. Greatness happens when you find your unique strengths and build upon them. Building up a weakness just makes you less disabled.

Building a strength can take you to the top of the world. Where would you rather be? When you discover a unique ability, there's no limit to what you can achieve.

I credit the adults in my life and the environment where I grew up with helping me find what I loved and excelled at. My parents' gift of a computer kit started me on electronics. My mother's uncle Bill and his tool kit introduced me to the world of machines when he helped me take apart my pedal car. My grandfather Jack bought me a Fender Showman amplifier and a bass guitar to start me off in music. Once grown-ups gave me a start I moved ahead on my own, but it all began with them.

Environment played a big part once I got moving. Since I lived in a college town there were really great resources at my disposal. I found well-stocked labs at the university and helpful faculty and grad students. My father taught philosophy there, so all its doors were open to me. To some extent the Internet makes knowledge available anywhere for today's kids, but there's no doubt that my location was a factor in my success, and that your location still matters today. There's a big difference between reading about something online and actually handling it in a university lab.

Every kid has areas of strength, and it's the job of grown-ups to help those kids find their unique strengths and then encourage them to develop them. Once I had my interests nailed down, I spent countless hours studying and practicing until I knew them cold. There were periods when I immersed myself in electronics and cars ten or more hours a day, seven days a week. There is just no substitute for that kind of concentrated practice.

I was very lucky to pick interests at fourteen that would last me a lifetime. Teens who know what they love and pursue it with single-minded determination have an undeniable advantage. If you look at the superstars in any field, you'll find people who took up their life's work as young adults. My friend Ron Feldman, for example, was the Boston Symphony's youngest cellist at nineteen. Bill Gates has written about immersing himself in computer programming as a teenager, which led to the formation of Microsoft a few years later.

When someone grows up to be successful, people are quick to say, "He just has an ability I haven't got!" But it's more likely that he found his area of interest and invested in it at a very young age. It's focus and hard work that truly bring success.

Find Real-World Applications for Your Special Skills

Right from the beginning I found people who appreciated my abilities and were willing to pay for them. You couldn't miss my special interests, because I seldom talked about anything else. For example, anyone could see my love of cars, and love of fine machinery. With all my enthusiasm, it's no surprise that folks would enlist me to fix their cars when I got older. My love of music and electronics was obvious, too, and that led to jobs working on sound equipment for local bands.

In both cases, my special interests were visible enough that opportunity came my way with relatively little effort on my part. One successful job led to another, and I took on more and more complex projects as my confidence and ability blossomed. Once I recognized that pattern I was able to continue seeking opportunities to earn a living doing what I loved. If my social skills had been better I might have progressed further and faster, but I still did pretty well with what I had.

Many people seem to go through life with the opposite perspective. They don't find their special interests, or ways to apply them. They reach the end of school with the question *What do I want to do?* unanswered. They pick a major in college, or select a trade, based on some arbitrary factors, like an uncle in the business or a magazine article or a recruiter who promised fame and fortune at his company. They lack a focus—a purpose—to their life. That's a problem I have never had.

Focus and Work Hard

Aspergian focus helped me become successful by allowing me to concentrate on my interests to the exclusion of all else. The tricky part was choosing productive things as my targets. If Apspergians can do that, there is really no limit to what we can do. My exceptional focus kept me on track, and my Aspergian brain helped me soak up new knowledge at a rate few nypical competitors could match.

Teenagers have a lot of time on their hands. It may not seem that way at age fifteen, but when you look back from the perspective of fifty, it's obvious. I had limitless energy when I was young. I'd get focused on something and stay at it till two in the morning, then get up at six and start all over again. Without really trying, I used that time to become a world-class expert in a few areas. And it's those areas of expertise that catapulted me to such success in my early adult years.

There is no substitute for hours and hours of practice. Music teachers say that about practicing the tuba or the bassoon, but it's true for anything. Whatever you want to be—an auto mechanic, an engineer, even a tracker of wild animals—you can't truly be an expert without putting in the hours. Asperger's can help you with focus and concentration, but we all have to put in our time.

Resolve

Resolve is another secret to my success. I'd like to paint this in a noble light, but a lot of my resolve is probably just common pigheadedness combined with Aspergian obliviousness. When I was young I would decide I wanted to do something, and more experienced older people would laugh and say, "You can't do that!" However, my Asperger's made me blind to their skepticism, which might have discouraged a nypical kid. So I went ahead, and many times, I succeeded.

Sometimes being oblivious of the skepticism and ridicule of others can be an advantage. When you combine that with my Aspergian way of solving problems, it can lead to some pretty striking accomplishments. And my focus keeps me going, even when it looks like I'm about to fail. I can stay the course, try again, and ultimately succeed—all because I'm too stubborn to do anything else.

Finally, I worked hard. And you can, too. Work those gifts for all they're worth.

Appendix for Parents, Teachers, and Others of Their Ilk

At this point, you have made it most of the way through the book without ever reading a definition of Asperger's or autism. That situation is about to change.

In this section, I define Asperger's and offer my thoughts on getting tested for neurological differences.

I have also put together an index of autistic behaviors and where they are discussed in this book. If you hear that a child has, for example, trouble with perseveration, you can use this index to see where that's discussed in *Be Different*.

Finally, I have compiled a list of further reading and resources.

Asperger's—the Definition

So what is Asperger's? I'll offer my insight interwoven with the "official" definition from the *Diagnostic and Statistical Manual of Mental Disorders* (DSM IV), which doctors and psychologists use. The main thing to understand about Asperger's is that it's a neurological difference—a difference in the way our brains are made. It's one of the conditions that doctors call an autism spectrum disorder, or ASD. In fact, in the upcoming edition of the DSM, due in 2013, Asperger's will no longer be listed as a separate diagnosis. It will be categorized as one of the autism spectrum disorders. There's no way to measure any form of autism with instruments—at least not yet—so a diagnosis must be made by asking questions and observing our behavior. There are six major points a doctor or mental health professional will look at when judging whether a patient has Asperger's or some other form of autism.

First of all, the person must have difficulty interacting with other people. I've listed four ways one might have trouble; the doctors say at least two have to apply for someone to be diagnosed.

A. The person might have difficulty with nonverbal behaviors like eye-to-eye gaze or reading facial expressions, body postures, and gestures. I sure had a lot of trouble with those. Things didn't really improve until I learned about my own Asperger's as an adult. But knowledge is power, and I've made huge headway with these behaviors today.

B. The person might not be able to make friends with kids his own age, at his own level. That's something I remember well from first grade—my total inability to make friends my own age. The kids in my class just laughed at me, and called me names like Monkey Face and Retard. There were two things that saved me from total frustration over that. First, some younger kids looked up to me. After all, any six-year-old is like a god to a toddler, even a friendless one like me. Second, a few adults stayed friends with me despite the strange things I said and did. Luckily, I've gotten past that and I now have plenty of friends my own age.

C. People with Asperger's often seem self-absorbed or uninterested in other people. For example, a classmate might say, "Look at my test! I got an A+," and the Aspergian might reply, "So what?" Anyone might react with total indifference every now and then, but acting disengaged and uninterested all the time is an indication that something may be up. Disconnection from other people and what they do is a sign of Asperger's.

This is a hard thing for people on the spectrum to work on, because while our self-absorption is innocent, others see it as malicious. It's not. We are simply oblivious of much of what goes on around us, because we are wrapped up in our own thoughts.

D. When two people approach each other, one often smiles, and the other smiles back, mirroring the first person's expression. One person might say, "Check out this new video," and the other person might answer, "Yeah, I've been wanting to see that one." Psychologists call that kind of behavior "social or emotional reciprocity." Often, people with Asperger's don't act that way. People smile at me, and I just look back at them with a flat expression. Someone might tell me about her video, and I'll say nothing.

I see myself in every one of those points. However, now that I'm an adult, I have learned how to adapt, and I've learned what other people expect of me. As a result, the differences that disabled me as a kid just make me ec centric as a grown-up. If there is a good side to life with Asperger's, it's the knowledge that we just get better with age.

That's not all there is to an Asperger diagnosis. In addition to poor interpersonal skills, the person must also have unusual interests, strange patterns of behavior, or fixations on objects. The diagnostic manual says that at least one of the four issues below must apply.

A. The person must have "an all-encompassing preoccupation" that is abnormal in intensity or focus. That's a mouthful, and it is kind of tricky to understand. I think this point is where many of our interests lie and where becoming a grown-up changes perceptions. For example, if you're ten years old and you can't talk about anything but carnivorous dinosaurs, you're abnormal. If you're the same way at thirty-five and a professor of paleontology, you are the smartest guy in your department. If you are fifteen years old and you can't think about anything but girls, you are normal. If you can't think about anything but light switches, you may be Aspergian. What that shows is that perceived mental health is sometimes just a matter of context and situation.

B. Alternately, the person might be someone who is stuck on what the doctors call "nonfunctional rituals or routines." Here's an example: You walk through the door of your school and immediately turn to check the potted plants by the door. You *have* to check to make sure that no one has thrown trash in the pots. If there is any trash, you *have* to get rid of it before entering homeroom. You go to the bathroom, get some paper towels, and then use them to pick up the trash without actually touching it so that you can throw it out. On your way to homeroom, you check every door you pass because the doors are supposed to be closed and you *must* make sure that rule is being followed. When you reach the bathroom near your own classroom, you go inside and make sure the light is on. You also make sure there are paper towels and toilet paper in case you need them later. You do your best, but you are always ten minutes late to class because you *must* do those things before going into your classroom.

That's the kind of routine they are talking about. It disrupts someone's life and causes issues with other people, and when you get right down to it, there's no purpose to it. I remember my little rituals well. Remind me to tell you about my pet trash.

C. The person might display stereotyped and repetitive motor mannerisms. For example, I used to rock back and forth endlessly. "Stop rocking!" grown-ups would yell at me, and I'd stop, but a moment later I'd start rocking again without even thinking about it. I always thought rocking was harmless to others and comforting to me, but it drove grown-ups wild. And that wasn't all. They'd also pick on me for twisting my hands a certain way, or tapping my foot in rhythmic patterns. Other people were convinced I did those things to drive them crazy, but it was really unconscious. I certainly didn't mean to be annoying.

I developed a whole host of strange mannerisms as a kid, but when I saw how they got me teased, I taught myself to control myself in public. For the most part, it worked. Some Aspergians learn to manage this pretty well; others don't.

D. The person might be preoccupied with parts of objects. Once again, the shrinks have said some "parts" are okay and others are "abnormal." A preoccupation with girls' legs is fine; a preoccupation with the differences between Standard and Kohler flush handles on the bathroom toilets is weird. If a guy talks about his female-leg fixation, all the guys around him will understand and chime in. If he talks about plumbing levers instead, those same guys will send him to the doctor. That's how we tell what's weird from what's normal. Weird preoccupations often get us into trouble.

Taken individually, those behaviors are harmless. But when a bunch of them occur together, and we are compelled to do them constantly, they can add up to a disability. It's all a matter of degree and control.

Psychologists talk a lot about rituals, how we struggle with them, and the ways perceptions of rituals change as we get older. Grown-ups jump all over us when we are kids, but when we become full grown others our age just look at us and say, "He's really set in his ways!" If our rituals are really extreme, they might say, "He's nuts!"

Everyone has eccentricities, but for those of us with Asperger's, those differences are a lot more pronounced. To get an official diagnosis, our behavioral aberrations have to cause significant impairments in social, occupational, or other important areas of functioning. As a child, my Aspergian behavior kept me from making friends and held me back in school. Therefore, when I was eight, a psychologist would have said that I had the disability of Asperger's. Later, my Aspergian brain helped me achieve unusual success in business and the creative arts. Today, I'm still Aspergian, but I am not disabled by any measure.

That's a very important point. Asperger's is a difference in our brains. It never goes away. However, as we get older and learn more skills, we can go from one extreme to the other—from disabled to gifted. That was hard for me to see at age sixteen, but it was obvious by age twenty-five. If you're struggling with Asperger's in middle school right now, no one can say how far you will go as an adult. All we can say is, life gets better for people like us. Often, a lot better. You may well surpass me in a few years. If you do, write a book so I can read how you did it.

Psychologists distinguish Asperger's from other forms of autism by our language skills. Kids with Asperger's learn to talk at the normal time, or even early. Most of us learn to say single words by age two, and we use phrases and simple sentences by age three. But that's just the minimum—kids with Asperger's often have unusually strong language skills, leading some people to call Asperger's the little professor syndrome.

By contrast, people with traditional autism usually have trouble with language. As toddlers, they often don't speak much, and if they do, they often have significant speech impairments. Some kids overcome the impairments as they get older, but for others it's a lifelong disability. It's a mystery why most kids with autism have trouble with language, but we Aspergians are often the opposite, with exceptionally clear and precise speech.

One day soon, science may give us a lab test that identifies people with autism or Asperger's. That would be great, because it would eliminate confusion and misdiagnosis, just the same way testing for blood type saves trouble in the hospital. But until then, we must rely on asking questions, making observations, and making a judgment based on experience.

Take the Test

Just the other day, a middle-aged fellow approached me and said, "I think I might have Asperger's. Do you think there is any point to my getting tested, or am I too old?"

I looked at him as I pondered the true meaning of his question.

"You do look pretty old," I said. "But I'll bet you could still take a test. Maybe they even have a simplified version you could try." I tried to look encouraging, but I'm not too good at stuff like that.

"That's not what I meant," he said quickly and with a hint of annoyance. "I was wondering if getting tested would serve any purpose!"

Now that his meaning was clear, I gave his new question more thought. Why do people get tested for neurological differences like Asperger's or autism? Most testing is done on kids, for a variety of reasons. However, it all comes down to one thing: Knowledge is power.

Knowledge may also be scary, but it is absolutely empowering. Without it, there is just fumbling and guessing.

My own life has illustrated that clearly. For my first forty years I was unaware I had Asperger's. I knew I was different, but I didn't know why, and that lack of knowledge suffused me with a feeling of inferiority that permeated and poisoned my life. Those feelings handicapped and hampered me in countless ways.

Learning that I was a perfectly normal Aspergian male (and not a freak) was a revelation that changed my life. Actually, "changed" is too mild a term. Understanding of Asperger's, and what flowed from it, turned my old life right on its ear and set me on a new and brighter path that I'm still following today.

If you are a teenager or even an adult who just feels different, the insight you can get from testing may be the best thing to ever happen to you. It can also be scary, but remember that whatever you learn about is already there, inside you. Self-knowledge can only be beneficial.

As for kids, they get tested when they don't do what's expected of them. For example, a tyke who doesn't talk when grown-ups think he should gets tested. A kid who never looks at people gets tested. There is this presumption in our society that all kids should talk and look at people, and woe to the toddler who fails to comply. If you're older and flunk out of school, you might get tested. If you don't act like the other kids, you are probably going to get prodded and measured until someone puts a name to your differences.

Of course, most testing of kids is initiated by observant grown-ups. Kids do not start the process on their own. I have never once heard of a first grader saying, "Mommy, can you test me for neurological differences?" In fact, I think it would be nothing short of remarkable to hear a question like that from a kid, even in today's enlightened times.

A six-year-old who gets tested probably can't make use of the results on his own. They'll be a big help to his parents and teachers, though, so the process is still important. A teenager is another matter. A fifteen-year-old can certainly take an Asperger diagnosis and run with it. He can read up on what it means and what he can do about it. A diagnosis can give a kid who wants to change his life a solid road map, and what better gift could there be?

There are some who dismiss the value of testing and diagnosis, saying, "Who cares?" Well, I speak from experience when I say I care. And many of my friends on the spectrum would say the same thing. There are others who say, "There's no such thing as normal!" To them, every single kid has a diagnosis waiting to be found. I understand their point, but I can't say I fully agree. If you are a person who struggles with some kind of disability, it's better to know what you're facing in the light than to struggle endlessly in the dark. Good test results can provide that illumination.

Psychologists believe that as many as twenty-five percent of the kids in our schools have some diagnosable disorder. Only a fraction of those kids get a diagnosis, though, and of that group, only a few receive any therapy or treatment. So lots of kids slip through the cracks, many Aspergians among them.

I didn't learn about my own Asperger's until I was forty, but the changes and growth I've experienced as a result of that insight are beyond words. And the same thing could happen to you or to someone you know.

I don't think there is any downside to being tested, but there are those who disagree violently with me. They say an Asperger or autism diagnosis can be devastating. There's some truth to that. It can be a blow, finding out you have a neurological difference that won't go away. But is living in ignorance better? I believe that no matter what the test results show, you will know more about your mind and the way it works. Testing is a tool to improve your life and make yourself more successful. And you don't have to be scared—the testing doesn't hurt much. There are no side effects.

When I talk about what testing and diagnosis have meant to me, I recall how they helped me understand exactly how my mind differs from other minds around me. For example, the simple insight that I miss nonverbal cues was life-changing. I seized upon the specific behavioral issues and set about constructing a better life. It worked.

Some people miss out on the benefits because they become sidetracked by preconceived notions about "having a diagnosis." Instead of looking at their own specific issues, they look at broad statistics associated with their condition. They see phrases like "thirty-two percent can't live independently" or "sixty-six percent never get married and have a family." Those numbers make them forget that they have power over who they become as individuals. They interpret those general statistics as a prediction for their own future, when it's nothing of the sort.

More specifically, they see their future as inexorably tied to every unfavorable broad statistic associated with their diagnosis. In that sense, some see an autism diagnosis as a sentence to some kind of living death. They get swallowed up by the negative features of their diagnosis, forgetting that they've lived their lives before and that life goes on after. In short, they allow themselves to become victims of a label.

That is the danger of diagnosis. Some people read what's associated with a label and make it self-fulfilling. They let go and become the worst of what they read. That negative outcome can be reinforced by teachers and adults who say or think, "He has a diagnosis of autism. We can't expect too much of him." That is most assuredly not the way I have lived my life.

It does not matter what sixty-six percent of people do in any particular situation. All that matters is what you do.

Other critics focus on the danger of a wrong diagnosis. Many parents have experienced this with their kids. They get referred for testing, and the first psychologist says the child has ADD. But then another round of tests with the next shrink points to PDD-NOS. More tests and more doctors take us back to ADHD, then Asperger's. They bounce from one diagnosis to another, never really knowing what to do or where they stand. In some cases, kids are given medications, and a medicine that's good for one thing can be bad for another.

That situation happens most often with very young children, most of whom don't have much input into their diagnosis beyond answering the questions on the test. Teenagers and adults are another matter. We can take a diagnosis, read up on it, and ask ourselves if it makes sense. If it doesn't, we can go back to the doctors and the test results and figure out why.

I agree that seriously wrong results can be worse than no results at all. But the same can be said of any kind of medical testing, and ultimately, all we can do is make our very best effort.

Most people go into testing in search of an answer, and most psychologists do their best to get the right result. You might say the shrink's job is similar to a car mechanic's. If you go in with a transmission problem and the mechanic overhauls your engine, you aren't going to be much better off than when you arrived and you'll be a whole lot poorer. Luckily, the skill level of psychologists is more consistent than that of auto mechanics.

How do you find a competent psychologist? Most people don't have the technical knowledge to evaluate a psychologist's skill. We must figure out another way to decide. For me, two words sum that way up: trust and confidence.

Whenever I need the services of a specialist in any field,

I ask him to explain whatever he proposes to do. I listen carefully to what he says, and I form an opinion about his abilities. *Is he able to show me what he wants to do? Is he ready and able to answer my questions? Is he really at ease explaining things to me, which tells me he really knows his stuff?* These questions apply to psychologists.

In my experience, competent people know how to explain themselves. That's an essential component of competence for most professionals. That's how I make my decisions about whom to trust, and I sharpen that with experience and the recommendations of others I also trust and respect.

Keep your local mental health workers employed, and improve your life at the same time. Take the test.

Index to Aspergian Behaviors

Discomfort in crowds is discussed in "Animal Wariness."

Failure to develop peer relationships is described in "Asperger's and Me" (on pages 10–11), "Finding Your Path to 'Fitting In'" (on pages 19–20), "For the Love of Routine" (on pages 29–30), "Making and Keeping Friends" (on pages 99–100 and 103–104), and "The Center of the Universe" (on pages 123–124).

Inappropriate expressions and responses are discussed in "Lobster Claws: Dealing with Bullies" and "Making and Keeping Friends" (on pages 100–101).

Frequent tendency to say things without considering the emotional impact on the listener is discussed in "Emotional Triggers" (on pages 92–93 and 96–97), "The Art of Conversation" (on pages 135–137), and "Getting Chosen" (on pages 155–157).

Impairment of comprehension, including misinterpretations of literal/implied meanings, is disscussed in "Mind Your Manners" (on pages 48–49) and "Emotional Triggers" (on pages 91–92).

Inability to recognize when the listener is interested or bored is discussed in "Mind Your Manners" (on pages 54–55).

Internalizing other people's problems—which is different from self-centeredness—is described in "Feeling Bad News."

Irrational fears are discussed and explained as perhaps not so irrational after all in "What Are You Afraid Of?"

Lack of social or emotional reciprocity is described in "(Not) Reading People."

Lack of varied, spontaneous make-believe play is discussed in "For the Love of Routine" (on pages 29–30).

Making friends is discussed in "Getting Chosen" and "Making and Keeping Friends."

Marked impairment in the ability to initiate or sustain a conversation with others and to see the point of superficial social contact, niceties, or passing time with others, unless there is a clear discussion point/debate or activity, is discussed in "Mind Your Manners" (on pages 55–56), "Getting Chosen" (on pages 154–155), and "Seeing Music" (on pages 173–174).

Peculiar names Aspergians give to people and things are discussed in "What's in a Name?"

Perseveration is described in "A Reason to Care" (on pages 60–61).

Restricted and repetitive patterns of behavior and interests are discussed in "Rituals, Manners, and Quirks," "For the Love of Routine," and "Learning Calculus" (on pages 205–206).

Seeing the world through different eyes is described in several chapters, including "A Day at the Races," "Seeing Music," and "Lobster Claws."

Self-centeredness and what it means are described in "The Center of the Universe."

Sensory integration problems are discussed in the chapters "Underwear with Teeth" and "Managing Sensory Overload" (on pages 181–182).

Socially inappropriate behavior is described in "Mind Your Manners," "For Love of Routine" (on pages 32–34), "A Reason to Care" (on pages 63–64), and "(Not) Reading People" (on pages 84–85).

Special interests and fixations are discussed in "Attention to Detail," "Learning Calculus," "I'm with the Band," "Finding Your Path to 'Fitting In'" (on pages 20–21 and 23–24), "What Are You Afraid Of?" (on pages 69–70), and "Seeing Music" (on pages 174–175 and 178–179).

Unusual language abilities that include advanced vocabulary and syntax but delayed conversational skills are discussed in "The Art of Conversation."

Unusual profile of learning abilities is discussed in "Learning Calculus" and "Plastic Brains" (on pages 225–226).

Unusual sensitivity is described in the chapters "Underwear with Teeth" and "Managing Sensory Overload" (on pages 181–182).

For Further Study

Autism Centers and Professionals
There are many good autism centers around this country.
All the places I've listed below are associated with leading
medical colleges and offer services ranging from behavioral therapies to testing and interventions. I apologize in
advance for not including more facilities; this list is limited to the small number of places of which I have personal knowledge through my work on autism grant review
boards.

UC Davis MIND Institute
2825 50th Street
Sacramento, CA 95817
(916) 703-0280
www.ucdmc.ucdavis.edu/mindinstitute/contactus/

Asperger's Syndrome and Autism Disorders Clinic
Beth Israel Deaconess Medical Center
330 Brookline Avenue
Boston, MA 02215
(617) 667-4074
www.bidmc.org

Mass General Hospital
YouthCare Programs for Kids and Teens with Asperger's
15 Green Street
Charlestown, MA 02129
(617) 726-0062
www2.massgeneral.org/youthcare/

University of Michigan Autism and Communication
    Disorders Center
1111 East Catherine Street
Ann Arbor, MI 48109-2054
(734) 936-8600
www.umaccweb.com/

Kennedy Krieger Institute
707 North Broadway
Baltimore, MD 21205
(443) 923-9200
www.kennedykrieger.org/

Thompson Center for Autism and Neurodevelopmental
   Disorders
University of Missouri
205 Portland Street
Columbia, MO 65211
(573) 882-6081
www.thompsoncenter.missouri.edu

Mount Sinai School of Medicine
Seaver Autism Center
1428 Madison Avenue
New York, NY 10029
(212) 241-0961
www.mssm.edu/research/centers/seaver-autism-center

The Children's Hospital of Philadelphia
Autism Center
34th Street and Civic Center Boulevard
Philadelphia, PA 19104
(215) 590-7500
www.chop.edu/service/autism-center/home.html

UW Autism Center
Center on Human Development and Disability
Box 357920
University of Washington
Seattle, WA 98195
Toll-free Information & Resource Line
   1-877-408-UWAC
(206) 221-6806
www.depts.washington.edu/uwautism/index.php

Appendix

University of California at Los Angeles Center for
   Autism Research & Treatment
Jane & Terry Semel Institute for Neuroscience & Human
   Behavior
300 Medical Plaza
Los Angeles, CA 90095
(310) 794-4008
www.semel.ucla.edu/autism

Yale Child Study Center
230 South Frontage Road
New Haven, CT 06520
(203) 785-2540
www.childstudycenter.yale.edu/index.aspx

You can find an updated and expanded version of this list on the www.johnrobison.com website. There is a much larger list of resources on the Autism Speaks website, at www.autismspeaks.org/community/resources/index .php, and on the Autism Society of America website, at www.autism-society.org.

Schools
There are a number of very different strategies for educating and socializing kids with autism. In my opinion, there is a place for every legitimate method because kids with autism are so different and varied. However, schools tend to adopt a single method like ABA (Applied Behavior Analysis) or RDI (Relationship Developmental Intervention), so a place that gets wonderful results for one child

may not succeed at all for another. For that reason, you should be prepared to try several schools with different approaches to see what works for you.

Two schools I worked with in the preparation of this book are Ivymount and Monarch. Ivymount School is located in Rockville, Maryland, just outside Washington, D.C. The Model Asperger Program there is run by Monica Adler Werner. If you are in the D.C. area and looking for a school for your Asperger's kid, you could not do better. Ivymount also has a well-regarded ABA program for kids with larger autistic challenges.

I've spoken several times at Houston's Monarch School, a place for kids with neurological differences. Monarch was the first school I visited where none of the kids had that hunted-animal look I knew so well from my own bad days in high school.

Support Organizations

I wish there were a solid national autism support organization for people on the spectrum, like AA for alcoholics. However, the current reality is that Asperger/autism support is local and highly variable. A few resources are listed here; I suggest you check the resources section of my website for the most up-to-date info.

The Autism Society of America is primarily focused on local outreach, with chapters all over the United States. Their regional and national conferences are really good, with presentations by Stephen Shore, Temple Grandin, Tony Attwood, and other respected people in the field. A list of local and regional chapters can be found on the national website, which is www.autism-society.org.

In New England we are fortunate to have the Asperger's Association of New England, online at www.aane.org. It runs support groups and seminars, and has an excellent annual conference.

The Global Regional Asperger Syndrome Partnership (www.grasp.org) sponsors support groups all over the country, with special emphasis on New York.

On Long Island, I admire the work of Pat Schissel and AHA. Find them at www.ahany.org.

In the Philadelphia area I like the ASCEND Group, online at www.ascendgroup.org.

Movies

In the introduction to this book, I mention the documentary film *Billy the Kid.* You can find the movie and the DVD through the website www.billythekiddocumentary.com.

A few other movies I recommend are:

If You Could Say It in Words: www.ifyoucould-movie
  .com
Temple Grandin: www.hbo.com/movies/temple
  -grandin
Autism Reality: www.autismreality.org
The United States of Autism: www.usofautism.com
Mozart and the Whale: www.mozartandthewhale.com
Adam: www.foxsearchlight.com/adam

Books

These first two books can give anyone (not just Aspergians) valuable insight into how to behave:

> *How to Win Friends and Influence People* by Dale
>   Carnegie
> *Etiquette* by Emily Post

This book will help you sort out what other people mean, by what they aren't saying:

> *What Every Body Is Saying* by Joe Navarro
> *You Say More Than You Think* by Janine Driver

People often ask me what my parents thought when I was growing up. My mother has answered some of those questions in her new book, *The Long Journey Home*. With the publication of her story, she joins me as a proud member of the Random House family of authors.

I always recommend the well-known works of Tony Attwood (*The Complete Guide to Asperger's Syndrome* and others) and Temple Grandin (*The Way I See It, Thinking in Pictures, Animals in Translation,* and others). There are the Daniel Tammet books, *Born on a Blue Day* and *Embracing the Wide Sky*. And there is *The Curious Incident of the Dog in the Night-Time* by Mark Haddon. In addition, these lesser-known books may be of help to you:

Atypical: Life with Asperger's in 20⅓ Chapters by Jesse A.
   Saperstein, a young Aspergian
Asperger's from the Inside Out by GRASP founder
   Michael John Carley
*Freaks, Geeks, and Asperger Syndrome: A User Guide to
   Adolescence* by Luke Jackson
Of Mice and Aliens: An Asperger Adventure (Asperger
   Adventures) by Kathy Hoopmann
Blue Bottle Mystery: An Asperger Adventure (Asperger
   Adventures) by Kathy Hoopmann
*Everybody Is Different: A Book for Young People Who
   Have Brothers or Sisters with Autism* by Fiona Bleach
Parallel Play by Tim Page
Songs of the Gorilla Nation by Dawn Prince-Hughes,
   Ph.D.
The Sensory-Sensitive Child by Karen A. Smith, Ph.D.,
   and Karen R. Gouze, Ph.D.
Alone Together by Katrin Bentley
The Thinking Person's Guide to Autism and its
   associated website, http://thinkingautismguide
   .blogspot.com

Every now and then, people ask why all the first-person
memoirs of life on the autism spectrum are by less-impaired
people. The answer is, more severely impaired people don't
write books very often. One exception is *The Game of My
Life*, by Jason "J-Mac" McElwain with the help of Daniel
Paisner.

There are plenty of memoirs from autism parents. Two that I like are

Making Peace with Autism by Susan Senator
All I Can Handle by Kim Stagliano

I also like *Gravity Pulls You In,* an anthology of stories about life with autism.

Web Resources

Barb Kirby and the people who created the *OASIS Guide to Asperger's* have a website with quite a few resources. Their site provides articles; educational resources; links to local, national, and international support groups; sources of professional help; lists of camps and schools; conference information; recommended reading; and moderated support message boards. The Web resources are in addition to the annual conference, newsletter e-mail, and phone support provided by MAAP Services. Find them at www.aspergersyndrome.org/.

My son, Cubby, and Alex Plank have a project called Autism Talk TV. In their films, they meet various people in the autism world and explore their stories. I'm proud of their efforts, which can be found at www.youtube.com/user/theWrongPlanet.

When Alex was seventeen, he decided to form an online community for young people on the spectrum. That community has grown to have forty thousand members and millions of page views each month. You can join at www.wrongplanet.net and visit Alex's personal site at www .alexplank.com.

Autism Speaks (www.autismspeaks.org) is the largest nonprofit organization in the autism world. It is dedicated to funding research to remediate autistic disability and of-fers some community outreach as well. I'm proud to serve on its Science Board, where we consider what studies we should be funding and how we can help people living with autism today.

My friend Stephen Shore is a renowned speaker and advocate for people with autism. He is at www.autism asperger.net.

Steve Silberman writes about autism and Asperger's, too, and can be found at www.stevesilberman.com.

And Now,
a Big Hand for the Orchestra . . .
Acknowledgments

My first book, *Look Me in the Eye,* was a fairly solitary effort. I didn't read any other similar books, because I didn't want my own writing to be influenced by anyone else. After all, it was my life story being related. I didn't expect that my book would become a guide for teaching Asperger's understanding and tolerance all over the world. I was flattered when that happened, but I was also worried. Had I given good advice?

Be Different is my answer to all those readers who asked for more insight. Since you asked me to think even harder than I had to for the first book, I felt I should get some help. I'd like to tell you about a few of those helpers and what they did.

First, I should thank the young Aspergians closest to me: my son, Cubby, and his Aspergian girlfriend, Kirsten Lindsmith. Cubby provided many of the story ideas, and Kirsten provided a female Aspergian perspective. And then there's our friend Alex Plank, who came to visit and never left. Alex and I did the train photography on the cover.

Acknowledgments

I have to thank my old friend Enzo DiGiacomo for providing the locomotives on the *Be Different* cover. I tell everyone they are my trains, but that's only because I bought them from Enzo! He has a collection that would be the envy of any railroad aficionado, and these two locomotives from his "grandchildren box" were just what I needed to replace the engines I had as a kid.

Another important contribution came from Louise Collins, who thought up the title *Be Different*. After all, what is any book without a title?

Dr. Kathryn James and the rest of the Communication Science and Disorders staff at Elms College in Chicopee, Massachusetts, deserve my thanks. Way back in the summer of 2007, Elms was the first school to adopt *Look Me in the Eye,* which it used in its brand-new graduate autism program. Today, I teach several courses at Elms, and I continue to serve as a spokesman for their graduate program. You can read more on the college website, which is www .elms.edu.

The autism program at Elms consists of classes on campus plus a Board Certified Behavior Analyst practicum at the River Street School in Coltsville, Connecticut. River Street specializes in helping kids whose differences preclude participation in mainstream schools. In particular, I'd like to recognize three friends from River Street for their support and encouragement.

Dr. Kathy Dyer works with kids at Coltsville. She has extensive experience describing autism in children, and she used that knowledge to create the index to behaviors in this book's appendix.

Rick Sadler, M.D., is the chief psychiatrist for the school. He's helped clarify my ideas about issues like medication and therapies for the severely impaired.

Dr. Mike Rice is River Street's head of psychology. He's helped me understand current therapies like ABA and RDI, and he, too, has been an invaluable source of ideas.

These doctors and I have talked through the issues facing teachers and schools today, and we've discussed my own issues and the stories in this book. They were kind enough to be early readers of this book to help spot the most egregious errors of fact or practice.

The next group I'd like to acknowledge are the brain scientists. In the winter of 2008 I was invited to join a research study at Beth Israel Deaconess Medical Center, which is a teaching and research hospital of the Harvard Medical School. I didn't have any previous experience with medical research, but I believed in the lab's director, Alvaro Pascual-Leone, M.D., Ph.D. Alvaro is the director of the Berenson-Allen Center for Noninvasive Brain Stimulation (online at www.TMSlab.org) and one of the premier neuroscientists in the world.

He recruited me into his autism studies, where we used TMS (Transcranial Magnetic Stimulation)—focusing high-power magnetic fields into the brain—to induce tiny electrical currents in my neurons, thereby altering the very way I think. Thanks to that work, I gained insight into the inner workings of my mind that few ever know. It's almost as if I had always been blind, and suddenly the scientists flipped a switch and I could see. From that moment, the world was different for me. My own disability was not as severe as blindness, but the effect of lifting the curtain was, for me, one of the most powerful experiences I have known. Research in the TMS lab offers tremendous promise; Alvaro and his team of scientists are truly pushing the envelope of neuroscience. I'm proud to have made a small contribution to their work.

Alvaro has provided advice and counsel, and insight into the workings of the brain that probably aren't available anywhere else. I've also been assisted by three of his brilliant staff, Dr. Lindsay Oberman, Dr. Ilaria Minio Paluello, and Dr. Shirley Fecteau. Together, they have introduced me to the wonders of neuroscience. It was they who explored the workings of mirror neurons with me, and I participated in some of their studies to unravel the secrets of brain plasticity. Thanks to them, I was able to experience personally the results I wrote about in the chapters on brain plasticity. More recently, my son, Jack, his girlfriend, Kirsten, and Alex also joined the TMS studies. The experiences I have had and observed in the TMS lab have influenced me as much as almost anything in my life.

Next I'd like to thank Monica Adler Werner, Bonnie Beers, Lisa Greenman, and the faculty of the Ivymount School in Rockville, Maryland, for their invaluable feedback about this book. They read early versions of the man-

Acknowledgments

uscript and gave me an educator's perspective on my story, something I didn't have before. In addition, they have provided one of the teaching guides that accompany *Be Different* (available on the Random House Academic website and at www.johnrobison.com).

John Barone and the staff and students at the Monarch School of Houston also made a big contribution to this work by exposing me to their thoughts and ideas. Monarch was one of the first schools to adopt *Look Me in the Eye,* and one of the first schools to ask me to speak to its students. From that beginning Monarch developed an excellent Leader's Guide for *Look Me in the Eye,* and I hope the school does the same for this book. Monarch's greatest gift to me is probably the student perspective. Much of the Leader's Guide was actually developed in conjunction with the students themselves; doing so was a remarkable experience.

I'd also like to thank the moms and teens who read this manuscript and offered suggestions. They read my stories, told me which ones were funny and which weren't, and offered their own ideas as to what the stories really showed. Some moms subjected my stories to actual kid testing, with their own children as readers. The book could not have reached its final form without them.

A few of the moms I'd like to acknowledge are Kyra Anderson, Drama Mama, Maria Polino, Kim Stagliano, Pam Victor, and Jess Wilson. These moms—and others I have not been able to name—continually amaze me with their energetic and tireless advocacy for their kids and kids in general. They have certainly given me the impression that moms of today perform at a higher level than the moms of my own childhood, though I'm sure those older moms would disagree.

Thanks to Mark Roithmayr, Peter Bell, Marc Sirkin, Geri Dawson, and the rest of the staff of Autism Speaks, for naming me to the organization's Science Board and thereby exposing me to some of the best minds in the world of autism science, therapy, and medicine.

I'd like to recognize all my geek friends and dads, folks like Bob Jeffway, Dave Rifken, Neil Fennessey, Rich Chedester, and all the rest who listen to my bizarre stories and come back with tales of their own.

My parents (including my stepmother, Judy) deserve mention for raising and partly civilizing me. My father died, but my mother and Judy are still with me.

I'd like to thank my ex-wife Mary for sharing the early part of my life and raising Cubby with me, and my ex-wife Martha, who still likes me enough to help with ideas and proofreading. I'm heartbroken that we failed to stay married but eternally grateful that we remain friends.

No acknowledgment for the recent past would be complete without a mention of the people who stood by Martha and me these past few years. I particularly want to thank Paul Picknelly and Bill Wagner. So much banking and business is impersonal, but those two friends put the numbers aside and reached out a helping hand without a moment's hesitation in our time of need. If the tables were ever turned, I would be proud to do the very same for them. I also owe a great debt of gratitude to Rick and Elaine Palmer, Gene Cassidy, Rick Colson, and all my other friends who were there for us. We would not be where we are today without all of you.

I'd like to recognize Ann Dawson, who was with me for part of this journey but chose a different path halfway through.

On a brighter note, I owe thanks also to my friend Jan Anderson, who talked through many of the ideas in this book and who continues to work with me setting up professional development programs in schools.

And I mustn't forget the crew at Robison Service—I depend on all of them to keep the company running when I am away. That's happened more and more in recent years, and I am so proud everyone at the company has risen to the challenge.

Thanks to David Lavin, Sally Itterly, and the rest of the folks at the Lavin Agency for their efforts to keep me out there speaking before colleges and organizations. Without that, I would not be exposed to the ideas that turn into stories.

Finally, I'd like to recognize Rachel Klayman, who began the editorial process at Crown, and Mary Choteborsky, who finished it. Then there is the rest of the team . . . Crown head Maya Mavjee; Tina Constable, who remains my publisher; Whitney Cookman, who made another fine book jacket; Lauren Dong, who returned to design the interior layout; Linnea Knollmueller, from production;

Acknowledgments

Robert Siek, from production editorial; Stephanie Chan, my assistant editor; Adam Goldberger, the copy editor; Linda Kaplan and Courtney Snyder, in foreign rights; Orli Moscowitz, at Random House Audio; Sarah Breivogel, in publicity; and everyone else at Random House who worked to make my books the successes they are today.

Back in my hometown, I want to thank the staff of Collective Copies of Amherst for their tireless work producing many intermediate copies of this book as I've created it. Even though the book was written electronically on a Mac, I still feel the need for real printed copies that I can refer to and mark up as I go along.

Then there's my younger brother, Augusten Burroughs. I would never have learned the art of storytelling if I had not had him as my very own captive audience long ago when we were children. Neither of us would be where we are now if not for Christopher Schelling, our friend and literary agent.

Last of all is a special thanks to Maripat Jordan for listening to my stories and understanding.

Woof.

John Elder Robison
December 2010

About the Author

JOHN ELDER ROBISON lectures widely on autism and neurological differences. An adjunct faculty member at Elms College, he also serves on committees and review boards for the Centers for Disease Control, the National Institutes of Health, and Autism Speaks. His previous book, *Look Me in the Eye,* was a *New York Times* bestseller and has been translated into ten languages. A machinery enthusiast and avid photographer, John lives in Amherst, Massachusetts, with his family, animals, and machines. Visit his website at JohnRobison.com.

ALSO BY JOHN ELDER ROBISON

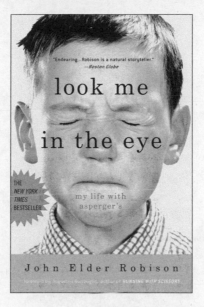

Ever since he was young, John Robison longed to connect with other people, but by the time he was a teenager, his odd habits—an inclination to blurt out non sequiturs, avoid eye contact, and dig five-foot holes (and stick his little brother in them)—had earned him the label "social deviant." It was not until he was forty that he was diagnosed with Asperger's syndrome. That understanding transformed the way he saw himself—and the world. A born storyteller, Robison has written a moving, darkly funny memoir about a life that has taken him from developing exploding guitars for KISS to building a family of his own. It's an indelible account—sometimes alien, but always deeply human.

Look Me in the Eye
$14.95 paper (Canada: $16.95)
ISBN: 978-0-307-39618-1

Available wherever books are sold.